PETA®

SHOPPING GUIDE FOR CARING CONSUMERS

SHOPPING GUIDE FOR
CARING
CONSUMERS

A GUIDE TO PRODUCTS THAT ARE NOT TESTED ON ANIMALS

PEOPLE FOR THE ETHICAL TREATMENT OF ANIMALS

PeTA

BOOK PUBLISHING COMPANY
SUMMERTOWN, TENNESSEE

PETA attempts to update this guide annually. However, we may not receive necessary information before going to print. Therefore, this guide is based on the most current information available at the time of printing. Companies not listed as cruelty-free may be cruelty-free but are not included because they have not sent PETA a letter stating their complete rejection of animal testing, nor signed PETA's Statement of Assurance. Companies identified as conducting animal tests may have changed their animal testing policies after this edition was printed. Inclusion on any list is not an endorsement of a company and/or any of its products by PETA. For periodically updated company information, please contact PETA.

PETA's updated 1999 *Shopping Guide for Caring Consumers* lists more than 550 cruelty-free cosmetics, household, and personal-care product companies, making it easy to find everything from hair color and furniture polish to correction fluid and more.

Inside photos by Jody Boyman

© 1998 PETA ISBN 1-57067-063-3

The Book Publishing Company
P.O. Box 99
Summertown, TN 38483

Edited by Susan Rayfield
Proofread by Karen Porreca

PETA
People for the Ethical Treatment of Animals
501 Front St.
Norfolk, VA 23510
757-622-PETA
www.peta-online.org

TABLE OF CONTENTS

Foreword 6
Introduction 7
Corporate Standard of Compassion for Animals 8
Animal Testing for Safety: Absolutely Unnecessary 8
Look for Vegan Ingredients 9
Caring Consumer Product Logos 9
Companies That Don't Test On Animals 10
Catalogs/Stores Offering Cruelty-Free Products 77
Quick Reference Guide 78
    Air Freshener 78
    Aromatherapy 78
    Baby Care 79
    Baking Soda 79
    Bleach 79
    Car Care 79
    Carpet Cleaning 79
    Companion Animal Care 79
    Condoms/Lubricants 80
    Contact Lens Solution 80
    Cosmetics 80
    Dandruff Shampoo 81
    Dental Hygiene 81
    Deodorant 81
    Ethnic Products 82
    Feminine Hygiene 82
    Fragrances for Men 82
    Fragrances for Women 82
    Furniture Polish 83
    Hair Care 83
    Hair Color 84
    Household Products 85
    Hypo-Allergenic Skin Care 85
    Insect Repellant/Treatment 86
    Laundry Detergent 86
    Laundry Detergent for Fine Washables 86
    Makeup Brush (Vegan) 86
    Nail Care 86
    Office Supplies 87
    Paint 87
    Permanents 87
    Razors 87
    Shaving Supply 87
    Skin Care 88
    Sun Care/Tanning 89
    Theatrical Makeup 90
    Toiletries/Personal Care 90
    Toothbrushes 92
    Vitamins/Herbs 92
Companies That Test on Animals 94
Alternatives to Leather and Other Animal Products .. 99
Health Charities: Helping or Hurting? 101
Health Charities That Don't Test on Animals 102
Health Charities That Test on Animals 112
Company Coupons 117
What Is PETA? 127

FOREWORD

Helping animals is now easier than ever before. Every time you buy shampoo, toothpaste, soap, and other cosmetics and household products from a cruelty-free company, you are saying "no" to the painful and outdated product tests some companies still perform on animals. More than 550 companies, including industry giants like Revlon, The Body Shop, and Estée Lauder, have signed PETA's Statement of Assurance or the Corporate Standard of Compassion for Animals, guaranteeing that they do not test ingredients or finished products on animals.

Sometimes products not tested on animals do cost a little more than other brands, but think of what you'll be saving: the lives of millions of animals who, without the actions of caring consumers like you, would still be subjected to Draize eye and skin irritancy tests and lethal dose tests. As consumer demand for cruelty-free products continues to grow, more and more companies are responding by using alternatives to animal tests such as tissue and cell cultures and computer models.

Many companies have also taken their commitment to helping animals a step further by using alternatives to animal ingredients. We encourage you to seek out vegan cosmetics and household products, and, to further assist you in living cruelty-free, please see the "Alternatives to Leather and Other Animal Products" section of this guide.

Please also see our new "Health Charities" section that lists charities that do and that don't fund animal experiments. Caring consumers who do not wish to contribute to health charities that conduct cruel animal experiments will find this information invaluable.

We have the power to speak out for those who cannot speak for themselves and demand an end to animal tests. By purchasing this book, you have taken the first step. The next step is to patronize the companies that are committed to producing safe, effective, and cruelty-free products—and to boycott those that aren't. With every cruelty-free decision you make, you will experience the satisfaction of compassionate living, and you will be demonstrating your respect for all life.

THE SHOPPING GUIDE FOR CARING CONSUMERS

We are pleased to present the ninth edition of the *Shopping Guide for Caring Consumers*. The information in this booklet was compiled by People for the Ethical Treatment of Animals (PETA) as part of its international Caring Consumer Project. PETA embarked on this project to offer consumers a way to identify products manufactured by companies that do not test on animals.

The companies listed in this shopping guide have signed PETA's Statement of Assurance or provided a company policy statement verifying that they:

1) do not conduct animal tests on ingredients or finished products;

2) do not contract with other laboratories to conduct animal tests;

3) will not conduct animal tests in the future;

and/or have signed The Corporate Standard of Compassion for Animals (see page 8) which, in addition to verifying the three requirements listed above, also requires companies to obtain statements of assurance from all their suppliers to the effect that no ingredients supplied to them were tested on animals.

7

CORPORATE STANDARD OF COMPASSION FOR ANIMALS

PETA and eight other animal protection groups recently formed the Coalition for Consumer Information on Cosmetics (CCIC) to create a unified policy in order to make it easier for consumers and companies to identify the products that meet ethical standards. This unified policy is the Corporate Standard of Compassion for Animals (CSCA). PETA is now encouraging all companies, including those that have signed PETA's Statement of Assurance, to adopt the CSCA. For more information on the CCIC or the CSCA, call 1-888-546-CCIC.

ANIMAL TESTING FOR SAFETY: ABSOLUTELY UNNECESSARY

Every year, millions of animals suffer and die in painful tests allegedly to determine the safety of cosmetics, household, and other consumer products.

Two of the most notoriously cruel and unnecessary tests are the lethal dose tests and the Draize eye irritancy tests, which, while still in use today, date back to the 1920s. In the lethal dose tests, animals are force-fed, injected with, or forced to breathe the vapor of toxic substances until a designated percentage of the animals die. In the Draize eye tests, a substance is introduced into albino rabbits' eyes, usually without anesthesia. The rabbits are immobilized in stocks, their eyelids held open by clips. The rabbits are forced to endure these conditions for up to 18 days. Reactions include discharge, inflammation, ulceration, hemorrhage, and blindness.

Not only are these tests widely criticized in scientific circles because of their cruelty, results from these tests are unreliable and often contradictory. Federal regulatory agencies such as the Food & Drug Administration do not require the use of animals to test cosmetics and household products.

Thanks to modern technology, many companies have turned to non-animal tests. Human volunteers, *in vitro* methodology, computer models, cloned human skin, tissue cultures, and extensive databases are just a few of the sophisticated, reliable alternatives available.

LOOK FOR VEGAN INGREDIENTS

Many consumer products contain animal-derived ingredients. Slaughterhouse byproducts are often used in hair and skin care products and even in toothpastes and shaving creams. Many consumers choose not to buy products that contain these ingredients because their purchase subsidizes industries in which animal suffering is inherent.

Our definition of vegan includes ingredients that are plant- or mineral-derived or synthetic.

Aside from slaughterhouse by-products, animal-derived ingredients include honey, beeswax, silk and silk byproducts, lanolin, and substances extracted from insects or sea animals.

Many ingredients can be of either vegetable or animal origin. These ingredients include, but are not limited to, cetyl alcohol, glycerin, lecithin, mono- and diglycerides, stearic acid, and squalene. If in doubt about the origin of an ingredient, please check with the manufacturer.

Companies marked with a **V** in the guide manufacture all product lines without animal-derived ingredients. However, most of the companies listed in the guide make some vegan products even if their line is not strictly vegan. Please check with the companies for further information on these products.

For a list of animal ingredients and their alternatives, please contact PETA's Literature Department at 757-622-PETA or www.peta-online.org.

CARING CONSUMER PRODUCT LOGOS

Since 1990, PETA has made the Caring Consumer Product Logo available to cruelty-free companies. You can be sure that products displaying this certified trademark adhere to PETA's stringent standards.

The Coalition for Consumer Information on Cosmetics (CCIC) has introduced a product logo in conjunction with the Corporate Standard of Compassion for Animals. As a member of the CCIC, PETA adopted this new logo in place of our Caring Consumer Product Logo. Please look for the new logo on cruelty-free products.

For more information about product testing or other animal rights issues, please contact:

People for the Ethical Treatment of Animals
501 Front St.
Norfolk, VA 23510
757-622-PETA

Companies That Don't Test on Animals

What Types of Companies Are on the "Don't Test" list?

The list includes cosmetics, personal care, household cleaning, and office supply product companies only. PETA'S Caring Consumer Project was founded upon the fact that no law requires testing of these types of products, so manufacturers of these products have no excuse for animal testing and should be boycotted in order to pressure then to change to a non-animal-testing policy.

The list does not include companies that manufacture only products that are required by law to be tested on animals (e.g., pharmaceuticals, automotive and garden chemicals, food additives, etc.). While PETA is opposed to all animal testing, our quarrel in this matter is with the regulatory agencies that require animal testing. Nonetheless, it is important to let companies know that it is their responsibility to convince the regulatory agencies that there is a better way to determine product safety.

The "don't test" list may include companies that manufacture both products that are and products that are not required to be tested on animals, but, in order to be listed, each company has stated that it does not conduct any animal tests that are not required by law.

Legend

- **V** Vegan. (Companies that manufacture strictly vegan products, i.e., containing no animal products. Companies without this symbol may still offer some vegan products.)
- ★ Company meets Corporate Standard of Compassion for Animals (CSCA).
- ▣ Company using PETA's Caring Consumer product logo. (All companies listed in the guide are cruelty-free. Many of them have chosen to use our logo to assist consumers.)
- **MO** Mail order available.

ABBA Products, Inc.
125 East Baker St., #120
Costa Mesa, CA 92626
714-885-9292
800-848-4475
Products: aromatherapy, permanents, skin care for men and women, bathing supply, shaving supply, soap
Availability: salons, beauty supply stores, boutiques, specialty stores
V 🐰

ABEnterprises
145 Cortlandt St.
Staten Island, NY 10302-2048
718-448-1526
Products: toiletries, household
Availability: mail order
MO

Abercrombie & Fitch
4 Limited Pkwy.
Reynoldsburg, OH 43068
614-577-6570
Products: fragrance for men, toiletries, personal care
Availability: Abercrombie & Fitch stores, Victoria's Secret stores

Abkit, Inc
207 E. 94th St.
Suite 201
New York, NY 10128
212-860-8358
800-CAMOCARE
Products: skin care, hair care, toiletries, household

Abra Therapeutics
10365 Hwy. 116
Forestville, CA 95436
707-869-0761
www.abratherapeutics.com
Products: aromatherapy, skin care, sun care, bathing supply, vitamins, herbs
Availability: health food stores, boutiques, specialty stores, mail order
V MO

Adrien Arpel, Inc.
720 Fifth Ave., 8th Fl.
New York, NY 10019
212-333-7700
800-215-8333
Products: cosmetics, skin care for men and women
Availability: department stores

Advanage Wonder Cleaner
16615 S. Halsted St.
Harvey, IL 60426
708-333-7644
800-323-6444
Products: household, carpet cleaning supply, furniture polish, oven cleaner, automotive cleaner, natural shaving lotion, hair care, multipurpose cleaner, aloe vera gel
Availability: Austin Diversified stores, distributors, mail order
V MO

African Bio-Botanica, Inc.
602 N.W. Ninth Ave.
Gainesville, FL 32601
904-376-7329
Products: hair care, skin care for men and women
Availability: beauty supply stores, mail order
MO

Ahimsa Natural Care Ltd.
1250 Reid St., Suite 13A
Richmond Hill, ON
L4B 1G3 Canada
905-709-8977
888-424-4672
AHIMSA@Interlog.com
Products: hair care, dandruff shampoo, fragrance for men and women, baby care, aromatherapy
Availability: health food stores, environmental stores, cooperatives, boutiques, specialty stores
V 🐰 MO

Alba Botanica
P.O. Box 40339
Santa Barbara, CA 93140
805-965-0170
800-347-5211
Products: hypo-allergenic skin care for men and women, sun care, toiletries, bathing supply, soap, shaving supply
Availability: drugstores, health food stores, cooperatives, boutiques, specialty stores, mail order
MO

Alexandra Avery Body Botanicals
4717 S.E. Belmont
Portland, OR 97215
503-236-5926
800-669-1863
Products: aromatherapy, baby care, condoms/lubricants, fragrance, hypo-allergenic skin care, sun care, toiletries, bathing supply, soap, shaving supply
Availability: mail order, health food stores, cooperatives, boutiques, specialty stores, salons
MO

11

320 lbs. of laundry miraculously cleaned by 32 oz. of cruelty-free liquid.

In one easy step you can help the environment, the economy and do your wash in the bargain. Because Allens Laundry Detergent is concentrated, it costs less per load than the leading brands.

Allens is powerful yet biodegradable, completely free of alcohol, phosphates and colorants. It's sensitive to your senses, containing no perfumes or dyes which are major allergy-inducing ingredients. And it's cruelty-free, meaning never animal tested and containing no animal products.

Now there's no need to compromise quality, integrity or effectiveness when choosing products that get the job done yet contribute to the health of our world. Allens Naturally home care products are the most powerful available but show a reverence for the delicate balance of our planet's fragile ecosystem.

Do your next load of laundry on us. For a free sample, write to: Allens Naturally, P.O. Box 514, Dept. GS, Farmington, MI 48332-0514.

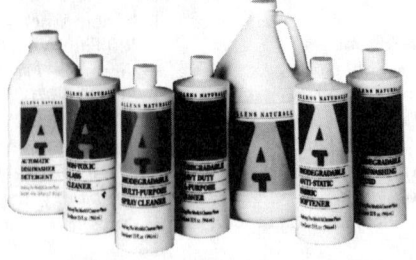

Making the world a cleaner place

Alexandra de Markoff (Parlux)
3725 S.W. 30th Ave.
Ft. Lauderdale, FL 33312
954-316-9008
800-727-5895
Products: cosmetics
Availability: department stores

Allens Naturally
P.O. Box 514, Dept. M
Farmington, MI 48332-0514
734-453-5410
800-352-8971
Products: household, laundry detergent
Availability: health food stores, cooperatives, supermarkets, mail order
V ★ 🌿 MO

Almay (Revlon)
625 Madison Ave.
New York, NY 10022
212-572-5000
Products: cosmetics, deodorant, hypo-allergenic skin care for men and women, sun care
Availability: drugstores, grocery stores, department stores

Aloegen Natural Cosmetics
9200 Mason Ave.
Chatsworth, CA 91311
818-882-2951
800-327-2012
Products: skin care
Availability: health food stores, cooperatives, mail order
MO

Aloette Cosmetics, Inc.
1301 Wright's La. E.
West Chester, PA 19380
610-692-0600
800-ALOETTE
102503.3221@compuserve.com
Products: cosmetics, makeup brushes, fragrance for men and women, nail care, skin care for men and women, sun care, toiletries, bathing supply
Availability: independent sales representatives

Aloe Up, Inc.
P.O. Box 831
6908 W. Expressway 83
Harlingen, TX 78551
210-428-0081
800-537-2563
Products: hair care, hypo-allergenic skin care for men and women, sun care, toiletries
Availability: health food stores, supermarkets, drugstores, boutiques, specialty stores, mail order
MO

Aloe Vera of America, Inc.
9660 Dilworth Rd.
Dallas, TX 75243
214-343-5700
Products: toiletries, skin care
Availability: distributors

Alvin Last, Inc.
19 Babcock Place
Yonkers, NY 10701
914-376-1000
800-527-8123
Products: hair care, dandruff shampoo, hair color (henna), dental hygiene, toiletries, shaving supply, cosmetics, skin care for men and women
Availability: health food stores, drugstores, mail order
MO

Legend
V Vegan (products contain no animal ingredients)
★ Company meets CSCA
🏠 Company uses Caring Consumer product logo
MO Mail order available

Amazon Premium Products
P.O. Box 530156
Miami, FL 33153
305-757-1943
800-832-5645
www.amazonpp.com
Products: Enviro-Magic brand, household, furniture polish, boat-cleaning supply, stainless steel cleaning supply for home, auto, and industrial use, teakwood cleaning supply
Availability: health food stores, hardware stores, marine stores, boutiques, mail order
V MO

American Formulating & Manufacturing
350 W. Ash St., Suite 700
San Diego, CA 92101
619-239-0321
Products: paint, stain, cleaners, adhesive, household, carpet cleaning supply, hair care
Availability: distributors, health food stores, "green" stores, building contractors, mail order
V MO

American International
2220 Gaspar Ave.
Los Angeles, CA 90040
213-728-2999
Products: skin care, toiletries
Availability: discount department stores, supermarkets, drugstores, boutiques, specialty stores, beauty supply stores, health food stores

American Safety Razor Company
P.O. Box 500
Staunton, VA 24402
540-248-8000
800-445-9284
Products: aromatherapy, toiletries, bathing supply, soap, razors, blades, shaving supply (Personna, Flicker, Burma Shave, Gem, Bump Fighter)
Availability: PETA catalog, department stores, discount department stores, drugstores, health food stores, supermarkets, boutiques, specialty stores, mail order
🏠 MO

America's Finest Products Corporation
1639 Ninth St.
Santa Monica, CA 90404
310-450-6555
800-482-6555
Products: household laundry and cleaning, laundry soil-stain remover, cool water wash for delicates, multi-purpose cleaner, concrete cleaner, elbow grease, liquid cleaner, water softener
Availability: supermarkets, drugstores, mail order
V MO

Amitée Cosmetics (Advanced Research Labs)
151 Kalmus Dr., Suite H3
Costa Mesa, CA 92626
714-556-1028
800-966-6960
aduva@advancedresearch.com
Products: hair care
Availability: supermarkets, drugstores, beauty supply stores

13

We never test our products on animals!

Amazon
Premium Products
featuring

Enviro-Magic®
Since 1978

Environmentally Safe Products for the World
1-800-832-5645   enviroworld@worldnet.att.net

Amoresse Laboratories
4121 Buchanan St.
Riverside, CA 92503
800-258-7931
Products: nail care
Availability: salons

Amway Corporation
7575 E. Fulton Rd.
Ada, MI 49355-0001
616-787-6279
www.amway.com
Products: baby care, animal care, cosmetics, dental hygiene, feminine hygiene, fragrance, hair care, dandruff shampoo, air freshener, household, bleach, carpet cleaning supply, laundry, sun care, vitamins, car care, furniture polish
Availability: distributors, mail order
MO

Ananda Collection
14618 Tyler Foote Rd.
Nevada City, CA 95959
916-478-7575
800-537-8766
tacjoy@nccn.net
Products: fragrance for men and women, household, air freshener, massage oil
Availability: drugstores, health food stores, cooperatives, boutiques, specialty stores, mail order
V MO

Legend
V Vegan (products contain no animal ingredients)
★ Company meets CSCA
🏠 Company uses Caring Consumer product logo
MO Mail order available

Ancient Formulas, Inc.
638 W. 33rd St. N.
Wichita, KS 67204
316-838-5600
800-543-3026
ancient@feist.com
Products: hypo-allergenic/acne skin care for men and women, herbal supplements for blood pressure, respiratory health, sleeping aid, carbohydrate balance, irregularity, prostate health
Availability: drugstores, health food stores, cooperatives, mail order, physicians
MO

Andrea International Industries
2220 Gaspar Ave.
Los Angeles, CA 90040
213-728-2999
Products: nail care, skin care for women
Availability: supermarkets, drugstores, mass retailers, discount department stores, boutiques, specialty stores

Apothecary Shoppe
P.O. Box 57
Lake Oswego, OR 97034
503-635-6652
800-487-8839
Products: aromatherapy, essential oil, herbs, homeobotanicals, flower essences, books, videos
Availability: mail order
MO

Aramis, Inc. (Estée Lauder)
767 Fifth Ave.
New York, NY 10153
212-572-3700
Products: fragrance for men and women, hair care, razors, skin care for men, sun care, toiletries, bathing supply, deodorant, soap, shaving supply
Availability: department stores, specialty stores

Arbonne International, Inc.
P.O. Box 2488
Laguna Hills, CA 92654
800-ARBONNE
www.arbonneinternational.com
Products: cosmetics, skin care
Availability: distributors
MO

Ardell International, Inc.
2220 Gaspar Ave.
Los Angeles, CA 90040
213-728-2999
Products: nail care, skin care for women
Availability: supermarkets, drugstores, mass retailers, boutiques, specialty stores, discount department stores

Arizona Natural Resources, Inc.
2525 E. Beardsley Rd.
Phoenix, AZ 85024
602-569-6900
Products: cosmetics, sun care, hair care, toiletries, baby care, hypo-allergenic skin care for men and women
Availability: distributors, discount department stores, drugstores, health food stores, supermarkets, boutiques, warehouse clubs, mail order
MO

15

A NATURAL TRADITION FOR 30 YEARS

Handcrafting 100% natural hair and skin care products—Aubrey Organics® has been doing it for the past 30 years. Over 200 completely natural shampoos, conditioners, hair gels, cleansers, masks, astringents, moisturizers, makeup, baby products and more. Preserved with citrus seed extract and vitamins A, C and E. Never tested on animals. Never warehoused. Catalog lists all ingredients. $2.00 (applied to first order). Order now and receive FREE cosmetic dictionary.

Look for us in better health food stores everywhere, or call 1-800-AUBREY H (1-800-282-7394) to order our full-color catalog.

AUBREY ORGANICS®

4419 N. Manhattan Ave., Tampa, FL 33614 • http://www.aubrey-organics.com

---

Aromaland, Inc.
1326 Rufina Cir.
Santa Fe, NM 87505
505-438-0402
800-933-5267
www.aromaland.com
Products: aromatherapy, fragrance for men and women, insect repellant, bathing supply, essential oil, aromatherapy books
Availability: department stores, drugstores, health food stores, cooperatives, boutiques, specialty stores, mail order
MO

Aroma Vera, Inc.
5901 Rodeo Rd.
Los Angeles, CA 90016-4312
310-280-0407
800-669-9514
www.aromavera.com
Products: aromatherapy, fragrance for men and women, hair care, air freshener, skin care for men and women, toiletries, bathing supply, soap, gift items
Availability: health food stores, Aroma Vera stores, boutiques, specialty stores, salons, spas, mail order
MO

Astonish Industries Inc.
Commerce Lane Business Park
423 Commerce La., Unit 2
West Berlin, NJ 08091
609-753-7078
800-530-5385
Products: household cleaning supply, air freshener, dishwashing liquid, carpet cleaning supply, antibacterial cleanser, sponges, laundry detergent, oven cleaner, nonscratch scouring pads, travel supply
Availability: drugstores, health food stores, supermarkets, specialty stores, mail order, QVC, The Shopping Channel
V MO

**Atmosa Brand
Aromatherapy Products**
1420 Fifth Ave., 22nd Fl.
Suite 2200
Seattle, WA 98101-2378
206-521-5986
206-621-6567
Products: aromatherapy, home fragrance
Availability: boutiques, department stores, specialty stores
[V]

Aubrey Organics, Inc.
4419 N. Manhattan Ave.
Tampa, FL 33614
813-877-4186
800-AUBREYH
www.aubrey-organics.com
Products: cosmetics, toiletries, hair care, baby care, companion animal care, fragrance for men and women, household, hypoallergenic skin care, sun care, shaving supply, deodorant, insect repellant
Availability: health food stores, mail order
[MO]

Aura Cacia, Inc.
P.O. Box 311
Norway, IA 52318
800-437-3301
info@frontierherb.com
Products: aromatherapy, baby care, fragrance for men and women, skin care, toiletries, bathing supply, soap
Availability: discount department stores, drugstores, health food stores, cooperatives, boutiques, specialty stores
[V] [MO]

Legend
[V] Vegan (products contain no animal ingredients)
[★] Company meets CSCA
[🐰] Company uses Caring Consumer product logo
[MO] Mail order available

Aunt Bee's Skin Care
P.O. Box 2678
Rancho de Taos, NM 87577
505-737-0522
Products: lip balm, skin care, personal care
Availability: health food stores, mail order, drugstores, supermarkets
[MO]

Auroma International
P.O. Box 1008
Silver Lake, WI 53170
414-889-8501
Products: fragrance for men and women, household, air freshener, dental hygiene, toiletries, incense
Availability: drugstores, health food stores, supermarkets, cooperatives, mail order
[V] [MO]

AUROMÈRE
Herbal Toothpaste
AYURVEDIC FORMULA

REQUEST A FREE SAMPLE

*T*he thirty natural ingredients in Auromère Herbal Toothpaste -- barks, roots, plants, flowers and essential oils -- have been indicated in Ayurvedic literature for centuries because of their natural efficacy in the care of teeth and gums.

Neem and **Peelu**, the two main ingredients in Auromère toothpaste, are renowned throughout India, the Middle East and Asia. "Chewing-twigs" from these trees play a part in the daily oral care regimen of millions, helping to whiten the teeth and promote strong, healthy teeth and gums.

Environmentally Friendly.
Cruelty Free.
All Natural.

Auromère toothpaste comes in three varieties.

Licorice
great tasting

Freshmint
for those who prefer mint

Mint-Free
homeopathically compatible.

AUROMÈRE Ayurvedic Imports
2621 W. Hwy. 12, Lodi, CA 95242   ph: 1-800-735-4691

Auromère Ayurvedic Imports
2621 W. Highway 12
Lodi, CA 95242
209-339-3710
800-735-4691
Products: dental hygiene, skin care for men and women, toiletries, bathing supply, soap, vitamins, herbs, ayurvedic, incense, massage oil
Availability: health food stores, cooperatives, New Age stores, mail order
V ★ ≋ MO

Australasian College of Herbal Studies
P.O. Box 57
Lake Oswego, OR 97034
503-635-6652
800-487-8839
achs@herbed.com
Products: aromatherapy
Availability: mail order
MO

Autumn-Harp, Inc.
61 Pine St.
Bristol, VT 04551
802-453-4807
Products: baby care, sun care, cosmetics, aromatherapy, nonprescription therapy, personal care
Availability: health food stores, cooperatives, drugstores, grocery stores, mail order, department stores
★ MO

Aveda Corporation
4000 Pheasant Ridge Dr.
Blaine, MN 55449
612-783-4000
800-328-0849
www.aveda.com
Products: cosmetics, hair care, skin care, "pure-fume" (R), lifestyle items
Availability: fine salons, spas, environmental lifestyle stores, health care facilities, educational institutions

Avigal Henna
45-49 Davis St.
Long Island City, NY 11101
800-722-1011
Products: henna hair color
Availability: health food stores, salons, specialty stores
V

Avon
9 W. 57th St.
New York, NY 10019
212-546-6015
800-858-8000
www.avon.com
Products: cosmetics, fragrance for men and women, hair care, dandruff shampoo, hypo-allergenic skin care for men and women, nail care, toiletries, sun care, Skin So Soft insect repellant
Availability: distributors, mail order
MO

Ayurherbal Corporation
1100 Lotus Dr.
Silver Lake, WI 53170
414-889-8569
Products: fragrance for men and women, household, air freshener, dental hygiene, toiletries, incense
Availability: health food stores, drugstores, cooperatives, boutiques, specialty stores, mail order
V MO

Ayurveda Holistic Center
82A Bayville Ave.
Bayville, NY 11709
516-628-8200
mail@ayurveda.com
Products: ayurvedic herbs for humans and companion animals
Availability: health food stores, ayurveda holistic center stores, cooperatives, boutiques, specialty stores, yoga centers
V

Bare Escentuals
600 Townsend St., Suite 329-E
San Francisco, CA 94103
415-487-3400
800-227-3990
Products: aromatherapy, cosmetics, fragrance, hair care, nail care, hypo-allergenic skin care, toiletries, bathing supply, deodorant, shaving supply, soap
Availability: department stores, Bare Escentuals stores, boutiques, specialty stores
MO

Basically Natural
109 E. G St.
Brunswick, MD 21716
301-834-7923
Products: aromatherapy, companion animal care, cosmetics, hair care, household, air freshener, bleach, laundry detergent, oven cleaner, insect repellant, hypo-allergenic skin care, sun care, toiletries
Availability: mail order nationally; local customers may choose from stock, by appointment
V MO

Basically Natural

For Your Healthy & Compassionate Lifestyle

No Animal Testing • No Animal-Derived Ingredients

Entire Vegan Product Line:
- Companion Animal Food and Care
- Household Cleaners
- Personal Care

FREE Mail-order Catalogue
109 East G Street, Brunswick, MD 21716

1-800-352-7099   *basnatural@msn.com*

Basic Elements Hair Care System, Inc.
505 S. Beverly Dr.
Suite 1292
Beverly Hills, CA 90212
800-947-5522
Products: hair care, skin care for men and women
Availability: salons, mail order
V MO

Bath and Body Works
7 Limited Pkwy. E.
Reynoldsburg, OH 43068
614-856-6585
800-395-1001
Products: aromatherapy, baby care, cosmetics, fragrance, hair care, household, air freshener, insect repellant, nail care, hypo-allergenic skin care, sun care, bathing supply, shaving supply, deodorant, soap, candles
Availability: Bath and Body Works stores

Bath Island, Inc.
469 Amsterdam Ave.
New York, NY 10024
212-787-9415
Products: aromatherapy, baby care, dental hygiene, toothbrushes, fragrance, hair care, dandruff shampoo, household, air freshener, nail care, skin care, sun care, toiletries, deodorant, soap, shaving supply
Availability: Bath Island stores, mail order
MO

Legend
- **V** Vegan (products contain no animal ingredients)
- **★** Company meets CSCA
- Company uses Caring Consumer product logo
- **MO** Mail order available

Baudelaire, Inc.
166 Emerald St.
Keene, NH 03431
603-352-9234
800-327-2324
Products: baby care, dental hygiene, hair care, hypo-allergenic skin care, sun care, toiletries, bathing supply, shaving supply, soap
Availability: department stores, health food stores, cooperatives, boutiques, specialty stores, mail order
★ MO

BeautiControl Cosmetics
2121 Midway Rd.
Carrollton, TX 75006
972-458-0601
Products: skin care, cosmetics, fragrance for men and women, nail care, sun care, hypo-allergenic skin care
Availability: distributors

19

Beauty Naturally, Inc.
P.O. Box 4905
850 Stanton Rd.
Burlingame, CA 94010
650-697-1845
800-432-4323
info@beautynaturally.com
Products: hair care, dandruff shampoo, hair color, permanents, hypo-allergenic skin care for men and women, deodorant
Availability: health food stores, mail order
MO

Beauty Without Cruelty Cosmetics
P.O. Box 750428
Petaluma, CA 94975-0428
707-769-5120
Products: aromatherapy, cosmetics, hair care, hypo-allergenic skin care for men and women, sun care, personal care, bathing supply, soap
Availability: department stores, health food stores, cooperatives, boutiques, specialty stores, beauty supply stores, salons, mail order
MO

Beehive Botanicals, Inc.
16297 W. Nursery Rd.
Hayward, WI 54843
715-634-4274
800-233-4483
beehive@win.bright.net
Products: dental hygiene, hair care, toiletries, vitamins, herbs
Availability: health food stores, mail order
MO

Beiersdorf, Inc.
BDF Plaza
360 Martin Luther King Dr.
Norwalk, CT 06856-5529
203-853-8008
Products: skin care, Nivea, Eucerin, Basis soap, La Prairie
Availability: grocery stores, drugstores

Bella's Secret Garden
6059 Sikorsky St.
Ventura, CA 93003
805-639-5020
800-962-6867
Products: toiletries, fragrance for women, baby care, hair care, household, air freshener, hypo-allergenic skin care for men and women
Availability: department stores, drugstores, boutiques, small gift stores

Belle Star, Inc.
23151 Alcalde, #A-1
Laguna Hills, CA 92653
714-768-7006
800-442-STAR
mickeylynne@msn.com
Products: fragrance for men and women, toiletries, incense, aromatherapy supply
Availability: Belle Star store, craft shows, boutiques, specialty stores, mail order
MO

Berol (Sanford Corp.)
2711 Washington Blvd.
Bellwood, IL 60104
708-547-5525
800-438-3703
Products: office supply
Availability: drugstores, supermarkets, office supply stores
MO

Better Botanicals
3066 M St. N.W.
Washington, DC 20007
202-625-6815
888-BB-HERBS
www.betterbotanicals.com
Products: aromatherapy, baby care, fragrance for men and women, hair care, skin care, toiletries, bathing supply, soap, herbs, ayurvedic
Availability: department stores, health food stores, cooperatives, Better Botanicals stores, boutiques, specialty stores, independent sales representatives, mail order, apothecaries
MO

Beverly Hills Cold Wax
P.O. Box 600476
San Diego, CA 92160
619-283-0880
800-833-0889
Products: cold wax, toiletries
Availability: health food stores, mail order
MO

Beverly Hills Cosmetic Group
289 S. Robertson Blvd., #461
Beverly Hills, CA 90211
800-277-1069
Products: cosmetics, fragrance
Availability: department stores, boutiques

BioFilm, Inc.
3121 Scott St.
Vista, CA 92083
619-727-9030
800-848-5900
lisaoc@biofilm.com
Products: Astroglide personal lubricant
Availability: drugstores
V

Biogime
10661 Haddington, Suite 160
Houston, TX 77043
713-827-1972
800-338-8784
Products: vitamin- and botanical-based skin care for men and women, sun care, toiletries
Availability: distributors, mail order
V MO

Biokosma (Caswell-Massey)
100 Enterprise Place
Dover, DE 19904
800-326-0500
Products: toiletries
Availability: specialty stores, mail order
MO

Bio Pac, Inc.
584 Pinto Ct.
Incline Village, NV 89451
800-225-2855
biopac@juno.com
Products: household, bleach, carpet cleaning supply, toiletries
Availability: health food stores, cooperatives, independent sales representatives, mail order
V ★ MO

Bio-Tec Cosmetics, Inc.
92 Sherwood Ave.
Toronto, ON M4P 2A7
Canada
800-667-2524
Products: hair care, permanents, hair color, skin care for men and women, toiletries, cosmetics
Availability: hair care in beauty salons, bath and skin care in retail outlets

Biotone
5747 Old Cliffs Rd.
San Diego, CA 92120
619-582-0027
Products: aromatherapy, massage cream, oil and lotion for massage therapists, hypo-allergenic
Availability: boutiques, specialty stores, independent sales representatives, direct to massage therapists, mail order
MO

Bobbi Brown
767 Fifth Ave.
New York, NY 10153
212-572-4200
Products: cosmetics
Availability: department stores

Bo-Chem Company, Inc. (Neway)
42 Doaks La.
Marblehead, MA 01945
617-631-9400
Products: household
Availability: distributors, mail order
MO

Body Encounters
604 Manor Rd.
Cinnamonson, NJ 08077
800-839-2639
www.bodyencounters.com
Products: aromatherapy, skin care, sun care, toiletries, bathing supply, soap, shaving supply
Availability: mail order
MO

Bodyography
1641 16th St.
Santa Monica, CA 90404
310-399-2886
800-642-2639
Products: cosmetics
Availability: beauty supply stores, salons

Body Shop, Inc.
1 World Way
Wake Forest, NC 27587
800-541-2535
www.the-body-shop.com
Products: aromatherapy, baby care, cosmetics, dental hygiene, toothbrushes, fragrance, hair care, hair color, nail care, razors, skin care, sun care, toiletries, bathing supply, deodorant, soap, shaving supply
Availability: The Body Shop stores, mail order
★ MO

Legend
V Vegan (products contain no animal ingredients)
★ Company meets CSCA
☒ Company uses Caring Consumer product logo
MO Mail order available

21

Body Time
1101 Eighth St., Suite 100
Berkeley, CA 94710
510-524-0216
888-649-2639
Products: aromatherapy, baby care, fragrance, hair care, air freshener, skin care, sun care, toiletries, bathing supply, shaving supply, soap, essential oil, massage oil and lotion, botanicals
Availability: Body Time stores, mail order
MO

Bon Ami/Faultless Starch
510 Walnut St.
Kansas City, MO 64106-1209
816-842-1230
Products: household cleaning supply
Availability: drugstores, health food stores, supermarkets, cooperatives

Bonne Bell
18519 Detroit Ave.
Georgetown Row
Lakewood, OH 44107
216-221-0800
www.bonnebell.com
Products: cosmetics, sun care, skin care, bathing supply
Availability: drugstores, supermarkets, department stores, discount department stores

Börlind of Germany
P.O. Box 130
New London, NH 03257
603-526-2076
800-447-7024
Products: cosmetics, hair care, toiletries, aromatherapy
Availability: health food stores, boutiques, specialty stores, salons, spas
★

Botan Corporation
3708 W. Broadway, Suite 1
Louisville, KY 40211
502-772-0800
800-448-0800
Products: hypo-allergenic skin care for men and women, toiletries, shaving lotion
Availability: health food stores, department stores, distributors, fine pharmacies, specialty stores, green boutique bath stores
V MO

Botanics Skin Care, Inc.
P.O. Box 384
Ukiah, CA 95482
707-462-6141
800-800-6141
Products: hair care, hypo-allergenic skin care, sun care
Availability: department stores, health food stores, cooperatives, boutiques, specialty stores
V MO

Botanicus Retail, Inc.
7610 T. Rickenbacker Dr.
Gaithersburg, MD 20879
301-977-8887
800-282-8887
Products: toiletries, fragrance for men and women, household, air freshener, hypo-allergenic skin care for men and women
Availability: department stores, drugstores, health food stores, Botanicus Retail stores, boutiques, mail order
MO

Brocato International
1 Main St., Suite 501
Minneapolis, MN 55414
800-243-0275
Products: hair care, dandruff shampoo, permanents
Availability: boutiques, specialty stores, salons
V

Bronson Pharmaceuticals
1945 Craig Rd.
St. Louis, MO 63146
800-521-3322
Products: cosmetics, vitamins, minerals, food supplements
Availability: drugstores, health food stores, mail order
MO

Bronzo Sensualé
945 41st St., Suite 202
Miami, FL 33140
305-531-2992
800-991-2226
Products: aromatherapy, lubricants, skin care, sun care
Availability: drugstores, health food stores, boutiques, specialty stores, spas, resorts
V ★ MO

Brookside Soap Company
P.O. Box 55638
Seattle, WA 98155
206-742-2265
Products: soap, companion animal care
Availability: health food stores, grocery stores in Washington, mail order
V MO

Bug Off
197 N. Willard St.
Burlington, VT 05401
802-865-6290
Products: herbal insect repellent for home, people, and companion animals
Availability: health food stores, cooperatives, sporting goods stores, veterinarians, environmentally friendly stores, mail order
V MO

22

KNOWING THE WONDERFUL BENEFITS THAT CARROTS PROVIDE...

health enthusiasts and beauty professionals all over the world are discovering the advantages of **BRONZO SENSUALÉ** Carrot Formula Health & Beauty Products. You immediately feel **BRONZO SENSUALÉ** assisting nature in rejuvenating your skin and keeping it smooth, soft, and protected. It does not turn your skin orange!

Based on proven European applications, **BRONZO SENSUALÉ**'s unique biodegradable natural formulas are created without animal testing nor animal ingredients; they are fortified with vitamins A, B, C and E, and antioxidants beta carotene, and glutathione; they contain skin-loving botanical remedies including the most sensuous natural oils derived from carrots, almonds, soybeans, sesame, and olives, blended with shea butter, aloe vera, allantoin, and non-animal lanolin; they contain a wonderful aromatherapy stress-relieving exotic plant fragrance of French lavender, Indian mint, Asian geranium, and Florida lemon & orange.

BRONZO SENSUALÉ Carrot Suntan Oils and Lotions replenish the moisture levels of the skin, neutralize environmental poisons, and resist damage due to free radicals, and come with a choice of Sun Protection Factors using sunscreens derived from cinnamon oil, Asian fruit tree bark, and natural crystals, helping to protect the skin from harmful UVA/UVB rays.

BRONZO SENSUALÉ
FOR THE SENSUOUS LOOK THAT GETS YOU THAT SECOND GLANCE.

For more information, visit our website: www.bronzosensuale.com
or contact BRONZO SENSUALÉ: 945 41st Street, Miami Beach, FL 33140
(800) 991-2226 • (305) 531-2992

23

Caeran, Inc.
280 King George Rd.
Brantford, ON N3R 5L6
Canada
519-751-0513
800-563-2974
Products: baby care, companion animal care, hair care, dandruff shampoo, household, car care, carpet cleaning supply, laundry detergent, hypo-allergenic skin care for men and women, toiletries, vitamins, herbs
Availability: health food stores, boutiques, specialty stores, independent sales representatives, mail order
MO

California SunCare, Inc.
10877 Wilshire Blvd., 12th Fl.
Los Angeles, CA 90024
800-SUN-CARE
Products: skin care for men and women, self-tanning products
Availability: salons

CamoCare Camomile Skin Care Products
207 E. 94th St., Suite 201
New York, NY 10128
212-860-8358
800-CAMOCARE
Products: natural skin care based on camomile, facial care, body care, hair care, feminine hygiene supply, toiletries
Availability: health food stores, cooperatives, nutrition sections in mass market stores

Candy Kisses Natural Lip Balm
16 E. 40th St., 12th Fl.
New York, NY 10016
212-951-3035
candykiss@beautycology.com
Products: cosmetics
Availability: mail order, discount department stores, drugstores, supermarkets
V ★ MO

Carina Supply, Inc.
464 Granville St.
Vancouver, BC V6C 1V4
Canada
604-687-3617
Products: hair care, dandruff shampoo, hair color, permanents, hypo-allergenic skin care for men and women, companion animal care
Availability: Carina Supply stores, salons, companion animal supply stores, groomers, veterinarians, mail order
MO

Carlson Laboratories, Inc.
15 College Dr.
Arlington Heights, IL 60004
847-255-1600
800-323-4141
Products: hair care, skin care, toiletries, vitamin supplements, natural personal care products
Availability: health food stores

Carma Laboratories, Inc.
5801 W. Airways Ave.
Franklin, WI 53132
414-421-7707
Products: Carmex lip balm/cold sore medicine, nonprescription therapy, personal care
Availability: drugstores, health food stores, supermarkets, mail order
MO

Caswell-Massey
121 Fieldcrest Ave.
Edison, NJ 08818
201-225-2181
800-326-0500
www.caswellmasseyltd.com
Products: aromatherapy, baby care, dental hygiene, toothbrushes, fragrance, hair care, skin care, toiletries, bathing supply, deodorant, shaving supply, soap
Availability: department stores, discount department stores, drugstores, health food stores, Caswell-Massey stores, boutiques, specialty stores, mail order
MO

CBD Enterprises
P.O. Box 4985
Chicago, IL 60680-4985
773-873-0500
www.fancybottoms.com
Products: disposable diapers, cloth diapers
Availability: mail order
V 🖾 MO

Legend
V — Vegan (products contain no animal ingredients)
★ — Company meets CSCA
🖾 — Company uses Caring Consumer product logo
MO — Mail order available

Celestial Body
21298 Pleasant Hill Rd.
Boonville, MO 65233
660-882-6858
800-882-6858
Products: aromatherapy, feminine hygiene products, hypo-allergenic skin care for men and women, toiletries, bathing supply, shaving supply, soap
Availability: health food stores, cooperatives, boutiques, specialty stores, independent sales representatives, mail order
MO

Chanel, Inc.
9 W. 57th St.
New York, NY 10019
212-688-5055
Products: cosmetics, fragrance, nail care, skin care, sun care, toiletries, bathing supply, deodorant
Availability: department stores, Chanel stores, boutiques, specialty stores, beauty supply stores

Chatoyant Pearl Cosmetics
P.O. Box 526
Port Townsend, WA 98368
206-385-4825
Products: skin care, toiletries
Availability: health food stores

CHIP Distribution Company
6120 W. Tropicana A16-357
Las Vegas, NV 89103
800-560-6753
Products: household, car care, carpet cleaning supply, oven cleaner, industrial/commercial supply
Availability: independent sales representatives, mail order
V MO

Christian Dior Perfumes, Inc.
9 W. 57th St.
New York, NY 10019
212-759-1840
Products: cosmetics, fragrance for men and women, skin care for men and women, nail care, toiletries
Availability: department stores, boutiques, specialty stores

Christine Valmy, Inc.
285 Change Bridge Rd.
Pine Brook, NJ 07058
201-575-1050
800-526-5057
Products: cosmetics, hypo-allergenic skin care for men and women, sun care, shaving supply, toiletries
Availability: salons, J.C. Penney stores, spas, mail order
MO

Chuckles, Inc.
P.O. Box 5126
Manchester, NH 03109
603-669-4228
800-221-3496
Products: hair care, hair color, permanents
Availability: salons

CiCi Cosmetics
215 N. Eucalyptus Ave.
Inglewood, CA 90301
310-680-9696
800-869-1224
Products: cosmetics
Availability: discount department stores, drugstores, boutiques, specialty stores, mail order, beauty and theatrical supply stores
MO

Cinema Secrets, Inc.
4400 Riverside Dr.
Burbank, CA 91505
818-846-0579
Products: cosmetics, theatrical makeup
Availability: beauty supply stores, salons, costume/novelty stores, Cinema Secrets stores, mail order
V MO

Citius USA, Inc.
120 Interstate North Pkwy. E.
Suite 106
Atlanta, GA 30339
770-953-3663
800-343-9099
Products: environmentally safe correction fluid, office supply
Availability: office supply stores, independent sales representatives, Sanford Corporation
V

Citré Shine (Advanced Research Labs)
151 Kalmus Dr., Suite H3
Costa Mesa, CA 92626
714-556-1028
800-966-6960
Products: ethnic products, hair care, dandruff shampoo, skin care for men and women
Availability: drugstores, GNC health food stores, supermarkets, beauty supply stores

Clarins of Paris
135 E. 57th St.
New York, NY 10022
212-980-1800
Products: cosmetics, hypo-allergenic skin care, sun care, nail care, fragrance for women, toiletries
Availability: department stores, boutiques, specialty stores

25

Clearly Natural Products, Inc.
1340 N. McDowell Blvd.
Petaluma, CA 94954
707-762-5815
cnatu31924@aol.com
Products: vegetable glycerin soap, liquid glycerin soap
Availability: health food stores, drugstores, supermarkets
V ★ 🐇

Clear Vue Products, Inc.
P.O. Box 567
417 Canal St.
Lawrence, MA 01842
508-683-7151
508-794-3100
Products: window cleaner, household
Availability: grocery stores in New England, mail order
V MO

Clientele, Inc.
14101 N.W. Fourth St.
Sunrise, FL 33325
954-845-9500
800-327-4660
Products: cosmetics, fragrance for men and women, hair care, hypoallergenic skin care for men and women, sun care, theatrical makeup, toiletries, vitamins
Availability: department stores, boutiques, specialty stores, mail order
🐇 MO

Clinique Laboratories, Inc.
767 Fifth Ave.
New York, NY 10153
212-572-3800
Products: cosmetics, fragrance, hair care, nail care, allergy-tested skin care, sun care, toiletries, bathing supply, deodorant, soap, shaving supply
Availability: department stores, specialty stores

Colorations, Inc.
2875 Berkeley Lake Rd.
Duluth, GA 30096
770-417-1501
Products: art and school supply for children
Availability: school supply, toy, and gift stores
V

Color Me Beautiful
14000 Thunderbolt Place
Suite E
Chantilly, VA 20151
703-471-6400
800-533-5503
Products: cosmetics, fragrance, skin care for men and women, sun care
Availability: department stores, drugstores, boutiques, specialty stores, independent sales representatives, mail order
MO

Color My Image, Inc.
5025B Backlick Rd.
Annandale, VA 22003
703-354-9797
Products: cosmetics, nail care, hypo-allergenic skin care, sun care, theatrical makeup, toiletries, bathing supply, camouflage makeup
Availability: Color My Image stores, mail order
★ MO

Columbia Cosmetics Manufacturing, Inc.
1661 Timothy Dr.
San Leandro, CA 94577
510-562-5900
800-824-3328
Products: aromatherapy, cosmetics, fragrance, hair care, nail care, skin care, sun care, soap
Availability: boutiques, specialty stores, distributors, mail order
MO

Comfort Manufacturing Co.
1056 W. Van Buren St.
Chicago, IL 60607
312-421-8145
Products: dental hygiene, shaving supply, skin care
Availability: beauty supply stores, department stores, drugstores, supermarkets, mail order
MO

Common Scents
128 Main St.
Port Jefferson, NY 11777
516-473-6370
Products: aromatherapy, baby care, fragrance, household, air freshener, skin care for men and women, toiletries, bathing supply, shaving supply, soap
Availability: Common Scents stores, mail order
🐇 MO

Compar, Inc.
70 E. 55th St.
New York, NY 10022
212-980-9620
Products: toiletries, fragrance for men and women
Availability: department stores

26

Compassionate Consumer
P.O. Box 27
Jericho, NY 11753
718-359-3983
800-733-4134
Products: cosmetics, toiletries, household, leather substitutes
Availability: mail order
MO

Compassionate Cosmetics
P.O. Box 3534
Glendale, CA 91201
Products: cosmetics, toiletries, perfume
Availability: mail order
MO

Compassion Matters
2 E. Fourth St.
Jamestown, NY 14701
716-664-7023
800-422-6330
Products: aromatherapy, baby care, animal care, cosmetics, dental, toothbrushes, fragrance, hair care, dandruff shampoo, household, air freshener, laundry, insect repellent, razors, skin care, sun care
Availability: Compassion Matters store, mail order
MO

Conair Corp.
1 Cummings Point Rd.
Stamford, CT 06904
203-351-9000
800-7-CONAIR
Products: Jheri Redding, hair care, hair color, permanents, toiletries, Conair hair care styling tools
Availability: discount department stores, drugstores, supermarkets, beauty supply stores

Concept Now Cosmetics (CNC)
P.O. Box 3208
Santa Fe Springs, CA 90670
310-903-1450
800-CNC-1215
Products: cosmetics, skin care for men and women, sun care
Availability: distributors, mail order
MO

Cosmair
575 Fifth Ave.
New York, NY 10017
212-818-1500
Products: cosmetics, fragrance for men and women, hair color, nail care
Availability: department stores, drugstores, supermarkets, boutiques, specialty stores
Note: Cosmair does not test its products on animals. It may, however, test its ingredients on animals.

Cosmyl, Inc.
1 Cosmyl Place
Corporate Ridge Industrial Park
Columbus, GA 31907
706-569-6100
800-262-4401
Products: cosmetics, fragrance for women, skin care for men and women, toiletries, nail care
Availability: J.C. Penney stores, Sears stores, department stores, boutiques, specialty stores

Cot 'n Wash, Inc.
502 The Times Bldg.
Ardmore, PA 19003
610-896-4373
800-355-WASH
Products: household, soap for fine washables
Availability: health food stores, cooperatives, boutiques, specialty stores, department stores, mail order
V MO

Country Comfort
28537 Nuevo Valley Dr.
Nuevo, CA 92567
909-928-4038
800-462-6617
Products: baby care, skin care, healing salve, lip balm
Availability: health food stores, cooperatives, mail order
★ MO

Country Save Corporation
3410 Smith Ave.
Everett, WA 98201
206-258-1171
Products: household, chlorine-free bleach, laundry detergent, automatic dishwashing powder
Availability: health food stores, supermarkets, cooperatives, select stores in Canada
V

Legend

V Vegan (products contain no animal ingredients)
★ Company meets CSCA
☒ Company uses Caring Consumer product logo
MO Mail order available

27

Countryside Fragrances
Pacific First Centre, 22nd Fl.
1420 Fifth Ave.
Seattle, WA 98101-2378
814-587-6331
800-447-8901
Products: potpourri, wardrobe sachets, essential oil, aromatherapy oil, simmering potpourri, mulling spices for cider and wine
Availability: wholesale to other companies, department stores, boutiques
V

Crabtree & Evelyn Ltd.
Peake Brook Rd.
Box 167
Woodstock, CT 06281
203-928-2761
800-624-5211
www.crabtree-evelyn-usa.com
Products: baby care, fragrance for men and women, razors, air freshener, toothbrushes, toiletries, shaving supply
Availability: Crabtree & Evelyn stores, department stores, boutiques, specialty stores

Creighton's Naturally
11243-4 St. Johns Ind. Pkwy. S.
Jacksonville, FL 32246
904-642-4591
800-969-4591
Products: hair care, dandruff shampoo, skin care, toiletries, bathing supply, deodorant, soap, shaving supply
Availability: department stores, discount department stores, boutiques, specialty stores, independent sales representatives

Crème de la Terre
30 Cook Rd.
Stamford, CT 06902
203-324-4300
800-260-0700
Products: hypo-allergenic skin care for men and women, sun care, toiletries
Availability: health food stores, boutiques, specialty stores, mail order
MO

Crown Royale Ltd.
P.O. Box 5238
99 Broad St.
Phillipsburg, NJ 08865
908-859-6488
800-992-5400
Products: companion animal care, fragrance for men and women, household, carpet cleaning supply, toiletries, shaving supply
Availability: grooming shops, distributors
V **MO**

CYA Products, Inc.
6671 W. Indiantown Rd.
Suite 56-191
Jupiter, FL 33458
561-744-2998
www.adzorbstar.com
Products: air freshener
Availability: health food stores, companion animal supply stores, distributors, boutiques, specialty stores
V **MO**

Dallas Manufacturing Co.
4215 McEwen Rd.
Dallas, TX 75244
214-716-4200
800-256-8669
Products: companion animal care
Availability: discount department stores, supermarkets, companion animal supply stores, wholesale, mail order
MO

Davidoff Fragrances
745 Fifth Ave., 10th Fl.
New York, NY 10151
212-850-2460
Products: Cool Water and Zino fragrances and ancillary products for men
Availability: department stores
V

Decleor USA, Inc.
18 E. 48th St., 21st Fl.
New York, NY 10017
212-838-1771
800-722-2219
Products: cosmetics, fragrance for men and women, hair care, dandruff shampoo, nail care, hypo-allergenic skin care for men and women, sun care, shaving supply, toiletries
Availability: department stores, boutiques, specialty stores, skin care salons, spas, Decleor stores

---

Legend

V Vegan (products contain no animal ingredients)

★ Company meets CSCA

🏠 Company uses Caring Consumer product logo

MO Mail order available

Pycnogenol®
50 times more effective than Vitamin E

Imagine what these Super Anti-Oxidants can do for your skin!

- Blended with Vitamins E, C & A.
- Helps Rebuild Collagen.
- Protects skin from free radical damage.
- Great for puffiness around eyes.
- Helps diminish the appearance of wrinkles, fine lines, brown spots & other skin irregularities.
- Promotes smooth, young & healthy looking skin.
- No Animal Testing.

To receive a Free Sampler Pack including 1/4 oz. Pycnogenol® Gel Send $4.95 Shipping/Handling to:

Derma E®

9400 Lurline Avenue, #C-1
Chatsworth, CA 91311
For Questions or Comments Call:
1-800-521-3342
http://www.derma-e.com

Deodorant Stones of America
9420 E. Doubletree Ranch Rd.
Suite C-101
Scottsdale, AZ 85258
602-451-4981
800-279-9318
dsa@primenet.com
Products: deodorant stones
Availability: health food stores, supermarkets, department stores, drugstores, mail order
V 🖃 MO

Dep Corporation
2101 E. Via Arado
Rancho Dominguez, CA 90220-6189
310-604-0777
www.dep.com
Products: Dep hair care, LA Looks, Agree and Halsa hair care, Lavoris mouthwash, Topol tooth polish, Jordan toothbrushes, Cuticura toiletries, Porcelana fade cream, Nature's Family, Lilt
Availability: drugstores, supermarkets, discount department stores, department stores

Derma-E Skin & Hair Care
9400 Lurline Ave., Suite C-1
Chatsworth, CA 91311
818-718-1420
800-521-3342
www.derma-e.com
Products: aromatherapy, hair care, dandruff shampoo, hypo-allergenic skin care for men and women, sun care, toiletries, soap
Availability: health food stores, beauty supply stores, mail order
MO

Dermalogica
1001 Knox St.
Torrance, CA 90502
310-352-4784
800-345-2761
www.dermalogica.com
Products: aromatherapy, skin care, sun care, bathing supply
Availability: skin care salons, physicians, spas

Dermatologic Cosmetic Laboratories
20 Commerce St.
East Haven, CT 06512
203-467-1570
800-552-5060
Products: baby care, hair care, dandruff shampoo, nail care, hypo-allergenic skin care for men and women, sun care, toiletries, bathing supply, soap
Availability: physicians, estheticians

Desert Essence
9700 Topanga Canyon Blvd.
Chatsworth, CA 91311
818-734-1735
800-848-7331
Products: aromatherapy, dental hygiene, hair care, skin care, toiletries, deodorant, soap
Availability: health food stores, boutiques, specialty stores

Desert Naturels, Inc.
74-940 Hwy. 111, Suite 437
Indio, CA 92201
760-346-1604
800-243-4435
Products: hypo-allergenic skin care for men and women, soap, Truly Moist products
Availability: drugstores, health food stores, cooperatives, distributors

DeSoto, Inc.
900 E. Washington St.
P.O. Box 609
Joliet, IL 60434
815-727-4931
800-544-2814
Products: private-label household cleaning supply
Availability: supermarkets, drugstores

Diamond Brands, Inc.
1660 S. Highway 100
Suite 590
Minneapolis, MN 55416
612-541-1500
Products: cosmetics, nail care, La Salle "10" nail treatments
Availability: drugstores, discount department stores, supermarkets

Dr. A.C. Daniels, Inc.
109 Worcester Rd.
Webster, MA 01570
508-943-5563
800-547-3760
Products: companion animal care
Availability: department stores, discount department stores, drugstores, independent sales representatives, companion animal supply stores
[MO]

Dr. Bronner's "All-One" Products Company
P.O. Box 28
Escondido, CA 92033-0028
760-743-2211
Products: castille soaps, baby care, companion animal care, hair care, toiletries, health foods
Availability: health food stores, cooperatives
[V] [★]

Dr. Goodpet
P.O. Box 4547
Inglewood, CA 90309
310-672-3269
800-222-9932
www.drgoodpet.com
Products: companion animal care, vitamins
Availability: drugstores, health food stores, mail order, companion animal supply stores
[★] [MO]

Dr. Hauschka Skin Care, Inc.
59C North St.
Hatfield, MA 01038
800-247-9907
Products: holistic skin care, hair care, cosmetics
Availability: drugstores, health food stores, cooperatives, boutiques, specialty stores, salons, spas

D.R.P.C. (AmerAgain)
567-1 S. Leonard St.
Waterbury, CT 06708
203-755-3123
Products: environmentally friendly, recycled office supply
Availability: office supply stores, "green" stores
[V]

Dr. Singha's Natural Therapeutics
2500 Side Cove
Austin, TX 78704
512-444-2862
www.drsingha.com
Products: aromatherapy, air freshener, bathing supply
Availability: health food stores, boutiques, specialty stores, mail order, spas
[V] [MO]

Earth Friendly Products
855 Lively Blvd.
P.O. Box 607
Wood Dale, IL 60191-2688
630-595-1933
800-335-3267
www.ecos.com
Products: hair care, household, air freshener, furniture polish, laundry detergent, personal care
Availability: drugstores, health food stores, supermarkets, cooperatives, mail order
[▨] [MO]

Dr. Goodpet

Naturally... it's the best.

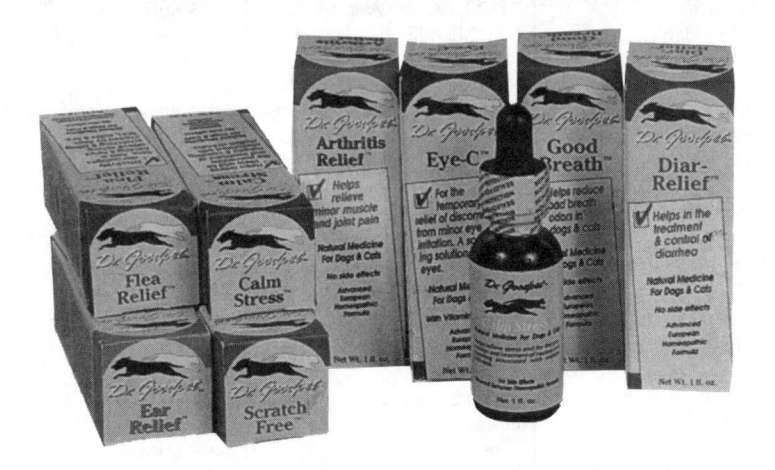

The Dr. Goodpet family of homeopathic medicines

- Natural Remedies for dogs and cats
- No side effects
- Flea Relief
- Scratch Free
- Calm Stress
- Ear Relief
- Diar-Relief
- Good Breath
- Arthritis Relief
- Eye-C

Dr. Goodpet
P.O. Box 4547, Inglewood, CA 90309
(800) 222-9932 Fax (310) 672-4287

Visit our website: www.goodpet.com

Earthly Matters
2950 St. Augustine Rd.
Jacksonville, FL 32207
904-398-1458
800-398-7503
Products: household, carpet cleaning supply, air freshener, furniture polish, laundry detergent
Availability: health food stores, distributors
V MO

Earth Science, Inc.
475 N. Sheridan St.
Corona, CA 91720
909-371-7565
800-222-6720
Products: aromatherapy, hair care, skin care for men and women, toiletries, bathing supply, deodorant, shaving supply, soap, vitamins, herbs
Availability: health food stores, cooperatives, mail order
★ 🖾 MO

Earth Solutions, Inc.
1123 Zonolite Rd., #8
Atlanta, GA 30306
404-525-6167
800-883-3376
Products: natural hypo-allergenic therapeutic skin care for men, women, and children, baby care, toiletries, companion animal care
Availability: health food stores, cooperatives, boutiques, specialty stores, independent sales representatives
V MO

Eberhard Faber (Sanford Corp.)
2711 Washington Blvd.
Bellwood, IL 60104
708-547-5525
800-438-3703
Products: office supply
Availability: drugstores, supermarkets, office supply stores
MO

E. Burnham Cosmetics
7117 N. Austin Ave.
Niles, IL 60714
847-647-2121
Products: cosmetics, hypo-allergenic skin care for men and women, hair care
Availability: health food stores, drugstores, mail order
MO

Ecco Bella Botanicals
1133 Route 23
Wayne, NJ 07470
973-696-7766
Products: aromatherapy, cosmetics, fragrance, hair care, dandruff shampoo, household, air freshener, hypo-allergenic skin care, bathing supply, shaving supply, soap
Availability: drugstores, health food stores, boutiques, specialty stores
MO

Legend
V Vegan (products contain no animal ingredients)
★ Company meets CSCA
🖾 Company uses Caring Consumer product logo
MO Mail order available

Eco-DenT International, Inc.
P.O. Box 5285
Redwood City, CA 94063-0285
650-364-6343
888-ECO-DENT
Products: dental hygiene
Availability: drugstores, health food stores, supermarkets, cooperatives, dentists
★ MO

Eco Design Company
1365 Rufina Cir.
Santa Fe, NM 87501
505-438-3448
800-621-2591
Products: companion animal care, dental hygiene, toothbrushes, furniture polish, laundry detergent, paint, wood finishing supply, hypo-allergenic skin care, bathing supply, shaving supply, soap
Availability: "eco" stores, mail order
MO

Ecover, Inc.
1166 Broadway, Suite L
Placerville, CA 95667
530-295-8400
800-449-4925
Products: household, bleach
Availability: health food stores, supermarkets, cooperatives, mail order
MO

Edward & Sons Trading Company, Inc.
P.O. Box 1326
Carpinteria, CA 93014
805-684-8500
Products: household cleaning supply, health food, hair care
Availability: health food stores, cooperatives, boutiques, specialty stores, mail order
MO

Lighten your skin and make age spots disappear -
safely, without dangerous chemicals

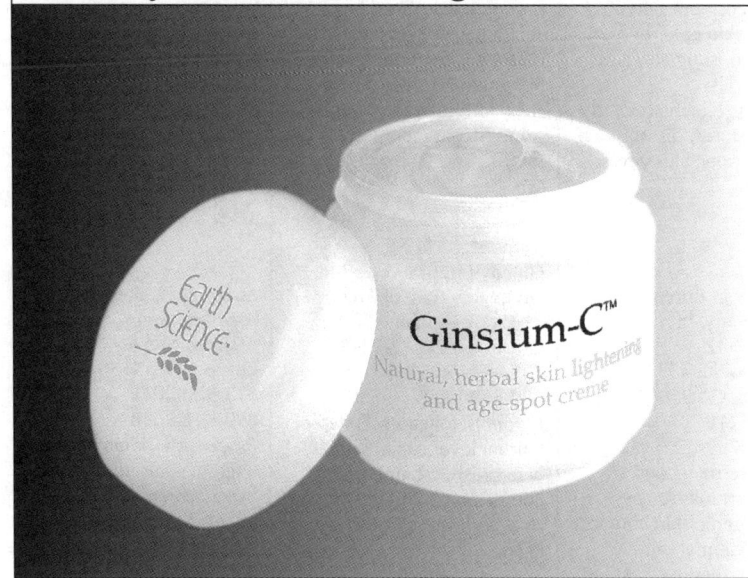

Lighten your skin to the shade you've always wanted, or safely rid yourself of those embarrassing age or "liver" spots. It's easy, with the natural herbal extracts in Ginsium-C fade creme.

The active ingredients are Magnesium Ascorbyl Palmitate (a mineral derivative of Vitamin C), "PTH" extract from natural Licorice Root, Ginseng and four other herbal extracts.

These natural extracts safely reduce the formation of skin melanin which darkens complexions and forms age spots.

We originally developed it to lighten the complexion of Japanese fashion models. After 3 years of test marketing, 95% of the women who used Ginsium-C lost their age spots or successfully lightened their complexion.

Contains no hydroquinone, a toxic chemical used in common bleach creams. No artificial colors.

Serious skin care™
from the laboratories of
Earth Science, Inc.
P.O. Box 1925
Corona, CA 91718 U.S.A.
1-800-222-6720

SAVE $2.00
Name (please print) _____
on
Address _____
Ginsium-C™
City _____ State _____ Zip _____
by
Favorite Nutrition Store _____ City _____
Earth Science®

Retailer: Earth Science will pay you face value plus 8 cents handling provided it was turned over to you toward the purchase of any Earth Science® product. Any other application constitutes Fraud. Invoices providing sufficient purchase of Earth Science products may be required to process claim. Coupon void where prohibited by law. Good in U.S. and Canada. For reimbursement send coupons to: Earth Science, Inc., Dept.   , P.O. Box 1925, Corona, CA 91718 USA. Limit one coupon per purchase. No cash value.

Elizabeth Grady Face First
200 Boston Ave.
Suite 3500
Medford, MA 02155
617-391-9380
800-FACIALS
Products: cosmetics, hypo-allergenic skin care for men and women, sun care, nail care, toiletries
Availability: Elizabeth Grady Face First stores, distributors, boutiques, specialty stores, mail order
MO

Elizabeth Van Buren Aromatherapy, Inc.
P.O. Box 7542
303 Potrero St., #33
Santa Cruz, CA 95061
408-425-8218
800-710-7759
evbsxinc@cruzio.com
Products: aromatherapy, hypo-allergenic skin care for women, essential oil, therapeutic blends, massage oil
Availability: department stores, drugstores, health food stores, metaphysical bookstores, massage therapists
V ★ MO

Enfasi Hair Care
927 McGarry St.
Los Angeles, CA 90021
213-488-0777
Products: aromatherapy, hair care, dandruff shampoo, toiletries, cosmetics
Availability: beauty salons

English Ideas, Ltd.
15251 Alton Pkwy.
Irvine, CA 92618
714-789-8790
800-547-5278
www.liplast.com
Products: Advanced Lip Technologies products, personal care, nonprescription therapy
Availability: beauty supply stores, department stores, salons
★

Epilady International, Inc.
c/o Beauty Care of America
39 Cindy La., Suite 300
Ocean, NJ 07712-7249
732-493-2435
800-879-LADY
Products: toiletries, Epilady hair remover, facial saunas, bath brushes, hair curlers, companion animal care
Availability: mail order
MO

Espial Corporation
7045 S. Fulton St., #200
Englewood, CO 80112-3700
303-799-0707
www.nomoreboss.com/products
Products: household, hair care, toiletries, skin care for men and women
Availability: distributors, mail order
V ★ MO

Essential Aromatics
205 N. Signal St.
Ojai, CA 93023
805-640-1300
800-211-1313
Products: aromatherapy, baby care, companion animal care, fragrance, hair care, skin care
Availability: mail order, select stores
V MO

Essential Oil Company
1719 S.E. Umatilla St.
Portland, OR 97202
503-872-8772
800-729-5912
Products: aromatherapy, baby care, fragrance for men and women, insect repellant, bathing supply, soap, essential oil, soap-making supply
Availability: health food stores, cooperatives, mail order, herbalists
MO

Essential Products of America, Inc.
8702 N. Mobley Rd.
Odessa, FL 33556
813-920-2011
800-822-9698
Products: aromatherapy, fragrance, air freshener, hypo-allergenic skin care, toiletries, bathing supply, soap, essential oil, vegetable oil
Availability: health food stores, boutiques, specialty stores, salons, spas, health care centers, mail order
V ★ MO

Estée Lauder Inc.
767 Fifth Ave.
New York, NY 10153
212-572-4200
Products: cosmetics, fragrance, nail care, skin care, sun care, toiletries, bathing supply, deodorant, soap, shaving supply, Clinique, Origins
Availability: department stores, specialty stores

European Gold
33 S.E. 11th St.
Grand Rapids, MN 55744
218-326-0266
800-946-5395
Products: sun care, hypoallergenic skin care for men and women
Availability: tanning salons, beauty salons, fitness clubs (where tanning beds are used)

EuroZen
10 S. Franklin Tpk., #201
Ramsey, NJ 07446
201-447-0961
Products: aromatherapy, scented massage oil, skin care
Availability: independent sales representatives, mail order
V MO

Eva Jon Cosmetics
1016 E. California
Gainesville, TX 76240
817-668-7707
Products: cosmetics, toiletries
Availability: health food stores, spas, specialty shops, mail order
MO

Evans International
14 E. 15th St.
Richmond, VA 23224-0189
804-232-8946
800-368-3061
Products: office supply, fingertip moistener, hand lotion, janitorial cleaning supply, household
Availability: office supply stores, office supply catalogs
MO

Every Body, Ltd.
1738 Pearl St.
Boulder, CO 80302
303-440-0188
800-748-5675
Products: aromatherapy, baby care, cosmetics, dental, hair care, dandruff shampoo, hair color, air freshener, bathing supply, massage oil, nail care, soap, shaving supply, deodorant, sun care, toiletries
Availability: Every Body, Ltd. stores, mail order, health food stores, supermarkets, cooperatives, boutiques, sports industry stores
MO

Face Food Shoppe
21298 Pleasant Hill Rd.
Boonville, MO 65233
816-882-6858
800-882-6858
Products: aromatherapy, hypo-allergenic skin care for men and women, toiletries, bathing supply, shaving supply, soap, acne care
Availability: Face Food Shoppe store, health food stores, cooperatives, independent sales representatives, mail order
MO

Faces by Gustavo
P.O. Box 102-149
2200 Wilson Blvd.
Arlington, VA 22201
703-908-9620
800-58-FACE1
Products: aromatherapy, baby care, cosmetics, hypo-allergenic skin care, sun care, toiletries, soap
Availability: Faces by Gustavo stores, boutiques, specialty stores, salons, mail order
MO

Facets/Crystalline Cosmetics, Inc.
8436 N. 80th Place
Scottsdale, AZ 85258
602-991-1704
Products: skin care for men and women
Availability: mail order
MO

Faith Products, Ltd.
Unit 5, Kay St.
Bury Lancashire BL9 6BU
England
161-7642555
Products: aromatherapy, hair care, laundry detergent, skin care for men and women, sun care, toiletries, bathing supply, deodorant, shaving supply, soap
Availability: health food stores, cooperatives, boutiques, specialty stores, mail order
MO

Farmavita USA (Chuckles, Inc.)
P.O. Box 5126
Manchester, NH 03109
603-669-4228
800-221-3496
Products: hair color
Availability: salons

Faultless Starch/Bon Ami
510 Walnut St.
Kansas City, MO 64106-1209
816-842-1230
Products: household cleaning supply
Availability: grocery stores, drugstores

35

Fernand Aubry
27, Rue de Caumartin
75009 Paris
France
01-49-26-00-80
Products: cosmetics, fragrance for men and women, nail care, skin care for men and women, toiletries
Availability: department stores, selected spas and salons, boutiques, specialty stores

Finelle Cosmetics
137 Marston St.
Lawrence, MA 01841-2297
800-733-9889
Products: cosmetics, fragrance for men and women, hair care, skin care for men and women, sun care, toiletries
Availability: distributors, salons, mail order
MO

Fleabusters/Rx For Fleas, Inc.
6555 N.W. Ninth Ave.
Suite 412
Ft. Lauderdale, FL 33309
954-351-9244
800-666-3532
www.fleabuster.com
Products: Fleabusters companion animal care, Rx For Fleas Plus powder
Availability: independent sales representatives, mail order, veterinarians, health food stores
★ MO

Flower Essences of Fox Mountain
P.O. Box 381
Worthington, MA 01098
413-238-4291
Products: vibrational medicine, holistic health care, nonprescription therapy
Availability: health food stores, bookstores, mail order, supermarkets
V MO

Focus 21 International
2755 Dos Aarons Way
Vista, CA 92083
619-727-6626
800-832-2887
Products: hair care
Availability: salons

Food Lion
P.O. Box 1330
Salisbury, NC 28145-1330
704-633-8250
Products: personal care, household
Availability: Food Lion stores

Forest Essentials
2144 Colorado Ave.
Santa Monica, CA 90404
800-301-7767
Products: fragrance for women, hair and skin care for men and women, sun care, toiletries, body and skin care gifts
Availability: environmental product stores, beauty supply stores, gift shops, department stores, catalogs
MO

Forever Living Products
P.O. Box 29041
Phoenix, AZ 85038
602-998-8888
Products: hair care, toiletries, dental hygiene, companion animal care, household, carpet cleaning supply, skin care for men and women, sun care, nutritional beverages
Availability: distributors, mail order
MO

Forever New International, Inc.
4701 N. Fourth Ave.
Sioux Falls, SD 57104-0403
605-331-2910
800-456-0107
www.forevernew.com
Products: advanced care formulations for fine washables
Availability: department stores, boutiques, specialty stores, mail order
V ★ MO

For Pet's Sake Enterprises, Inc.
3780 Eastway Rd., Suite 10A
South Euclid, OH 44118
216-932-8810
800-285-0298
76460.1266@compuserve.com
Products: aromatherapy, baby care, cosmetics, fragrance, hair care, dandruff shampoo, household, nail care, skin care, toiletries, vitamins, deodorant, car care
Availability: mail order, distributors
MO

Fragrance Impressions, Ltd.
116 Knowlton St.
Bridgeport, CT 06608
203-367-6995
800-541-3204
Products: fragrance for men and women
Availability: drugstores, supermarkets

Framesi USA, Inc.
400 Chess St.
Coraopolis, PA 15108
412-269-2950
800-321-9648
Products: hair care, hair color, permanents
Availability: salons

Freeda Vitamins, Inc.
36 E. 41st St.
New York, NY 10017
212-685-4980
800-777-3737
Products: vitamins and nutrients
Availability: health food stores, drugstores, cooperatives, Freeda Vitamin stores, mail order
Note: 20 percent discount to PETA members
V MO

Freeman Cosmetic Corporation
10000 Santa Monica Blvd. #400
Los Angeles, CA 90067
310-286-0101
www.freemancosmetics.com
Products: hair care, skin care and bathing supply for men and women, sun care
Availability: drugstores, supermarkets, beauty supply stores

Free Spirit Enterprises, Inc.
P.O. Box 2638
Guerneville, CA 95446
707-869-1942
Products: skin care, toiletries, personal care, massage lotion
Availability: department stores, drugstores, health food stores, supermarkets, cooperatives, boutiques, specialty stores, mail order
V MO

French Transit
398 Beach Rd.
Burlingame, CA 94010
415-548-9000
800-829-7625
www.thecrystal.com
Products: deodorant
Availability: department stores, drugstores, supermarkets, health food stores, mail order
V ★ MO

Frontier Natural Products Co-op
3021 78th St.
Box 299
Norway, IA 52318
319-227-7996
800-669-3275
Products: aromatherapy, fragrance, household, baking soda, toiletries, bathing supply, soap, vitamins, herbs
Availability: health food stores, cooperatives, mail order
V MO

Fruit of the Earth, Inc.
P.O. Box 152044
Irving, TX 75015-2044
972-790-0808
800-527-7731
Products: sun care, skin care, hair care
Availability: drugstores, supermarkets, discount department stores

Garden Botanika
8624 154th Ave. N.E.
Redmond, WA 98052
425-881-9603
800-968-7842
www.gardenbotanika.com
Products: cosmetics, fragrance, hair care, nail care, hypo-allergenic skin care, sun care, toiletries, bathing supply, deodorant, shaving supply, soap
Availability: Garden Botanika stores, mail order
MO

Garnier (L'Oréal)
575 Fifth Ave.
New York, NY 10017
212-818-1500
Products: hair color
Availability: supermarkets, drugstores
Note: Garnier does not test its products on animals. It may, however, test its ingredients on animals.

Georgette Klinger, Inc.
501 Madison Ave.
New York, NY 10022
212-838-3200
800-KLINGER
Products: cosmetics, fragrance for men and women, hair care, nail care, skin care, sun care, toiletries, bathing supply, soap, shaving supply
Availability: Georgette Klinger salons, specialty stores, mail order
MO

Gigi Laboratories
2220 Gaspar Ave.
Los Angeles, CA 90040
213-728-2999
Products: skin care for women
Availability: boutiques, specialty stores, beauty supply stores

37

I DON'T CARE ABOUT THE POOR
I DON'T CARE ABOUT THE SICK
I DON'T CARE ABOUT THE HOMELESS
I DON'T CARE ABOUT THE ANIMALS
I DON'T CARE ABOUT THEIR PAIN
I DON'T CARE ABOUT LOOKING CRASS
I DON'T CARE ABOUT THE EARTH

I WEAR FUR BECAUSE
I DON'T CARE

If you **DO** care about something other than your own vanity, contact us and we'll show you how we can all share in a better world.

PeTA PEOPLE FOR THE ETHICAL TREATMENT OF ANIMALS
501 FRONT ST., NORFOLK, VA 23510 ☎ 757-622-PETA

Giovanni Cosmetics, Inc.
5415 Tweedy Blvd.
Southgate, CA 90280
213-563-0355
800-563-5468
Products: hair care
Availability: health food stores, cooperatives, mail order
V MO

Golden Pride/Rawleigh, Inc.
1501 Northpoint Pkwy.
Suite 100
West Palm Beach, FL 33407
407-640-5700
Products: household, furniture polish, laundry detergent, vitamins
Availability: distributors, mail order
MO

Goldwell Cosmetics (USA), Inc.
981 Corporate Blvd.
Linthicum, MD 21090
301-725-6620
800-288-9118
Products: hair care, hair color
Availability: salons

Green Ban
P.O. Box 146
Norway, IA 52318
319-446-7495
Products: companion animal care, insect repellant, insect-bite treatment
Availability: health food stores, cooperatives, specialty stores, camping outlets, mail order
V MO

Greentree Laboratories, Inc.
P.O. Box 425
Tustin, CA 92681
714-546-9520
Products: companion animal care
Availability: companion animal supply stores, mail order
MO

Greenway Products
P.O. Box 183
Port Townsend, WA 98368
800-966-1445
Products: household, toiletries, companion animal care, hair care, carpet cleaning supply, hypo-allergenic skin care for men and women, shaving supply, accessories and promotional items
Availability: distributors, mail order
V MO

Gryphon Development
666 Fifth Ave.
New York, NY 10103
212-582-1220
Products: Victoria's Secret, Bath & Body Works, Abercrombie & Fitch, Henri Bendel, toiletries, personal care, fragrance
Availability: Victoria's Secret, Bath & Body Works, Abercrombie & Fitch, Henri Bendel

Gucci Parfums
15 Executive Blvd.
Orange, CT 06477
Products: fragrance for men and women, toiletries, shaving supply, skin care
Availability: department stores

Halo Purely for Pets
3438 E. Lake Rd., #14
Palm Harbor, FL 34685
813-854-2214
Products: companion animal care
Availability: companion animal supply stores, health food stores, mail order
MO

Hard Candy, Inc.
110 N. Doheny Dr.
Beverly Hills, CA 90211
310-275-8099
Products: cosmetics, nail care
Availability: department stores, boutiques

Hargen Distributing, Inc.
4015 N. 40th Place
Phoenix, AZ 85018
602-381-0799
Products: deodorant stones
Availability: health food stores, mail order
V MO

Harvey Universal Environmental Products
15948 Downey Ave.
Paramount, CA 90723
310-328-9000
800-800-3330
Products: household and industrial cleaning supply, carpet cleaning supply, air freshener
Availability: health food stores, distributors, companion animal supply stores, supermarkets, cooperatives, boutiques, specialty stores, home centers, mail order
V MO

39

Hawaiian Resources Co., Ltd.
P.O. Box 1059
Wahiawa, HI 96786
808-621-6270
Products: personal care, sun care
Availability: drugstores, health food stores, mail order
V ★

Healthy Times
461 Vernon Way
El Cajon, CA 92020
619-593-2229
Products: baby care
Availability: health food stores, cooperatives, mail order, baby supply stores
V MO

Helen Lee Skin Care and Cosmetics
205 E. 60th St.
New York, NY 10022
212-888-1233
800-288-1077
Products: cosmetics, hair care, hypo-allergenic skin care for men and women, vitamins, herbs
Availability: Helen Lee Day Spas, mail order
MO

Henri Bendel
712 Fifth Ave.
New York, NY 10019
212-247-1100
Products: fragrance for women
Availability: Henri Bendel stores, mail order
MO

Herbal Products & Development
P.O. Box 1084
Aptos, CA 95001
408-688-8706
herbalproducts@pacifichemp.com
Products: air freshener, insect repellant, vitamins, herbs, whole food and herbal concentrates
Availability: health food stores, independent sales representatives, mail order
★ MO

Herb Garden
P.O. Box 773-P
Pilot Mountain, NC 27041
910-368-2723
Products: aromatherapy, companion animal care, fragrance, insect repellant, skin care, soap, vitamins, herbs
Availability: mail order, farmers' markets
V MO

H.e.r.c. Consumer Products
2538 N. Sandy Creek Dr.
Westlake Village, CA 91361
818-991-9985
Products: household
Availability: health food stores, home centers and hardware stores, mail order
V MO

Hewitt Soap Company, Inc.
333 Linden Ave.
Dayton, OH 45403
513-253-1151
800-543-2245
Products: companion animal care, fragrance for men and women, toiletries
Availability: health food stores, drugstores, department stores, discount department stores, boutiques, specialty stores, distributors, mail order
MO

Hobé Laboratories, Inc.
4032 E. Broadway
Phoenix, AZ 85040
602-257-1950
800-528-4482
Products: hair care, skin care for men and women, hair loss and scalp problem shampoo, psoriasis treatment, supplements, weight loss tea, topical analgesic, instant surface sanitizers
Availability: department stores, drugstores, health food stores, supermarkets, cooperatives, boutiques, specialty stores, mail order
MO

Homebody (Perfumoils, Inc.)
143A Main St.
Brattleboro, VT 05301
802-254-6280
Products: toiletries, fragrance for men and women, shaving supply, hypo-allergenic skin care for men and women, glycerin soap, hair care
Availability: Homebody stores

Home Health Products, Inc.
P.O. Box 8425
Virginia Beach, VA 23450
757-468-3130
800-284-9123
Products: aromatherapy, companion animal care, dental hygiene, hair care, dandruff shampoo, household, feminine hygiene, insect repellant, nail care, skin care, toiletries, vitamins
Availability: health food stores, cooperatives, mail order
MO

Home Service Products Company
P.O. Box 129
Lambertville, NJ 08530
609-397-8674
Products: Professional Brand, laundry detergent, bleach, household
Availability: independent sales representatives, mail order
V ★ MO

House of Cheriss
13475 Holiday Dr.
Saratoga, CA 95070
408-867-6795
Products: ayurvedic skin care for men and women, cleansing cream, washing grains, toner, moisturizer, body lotion, hair oil, travel packs, massage cream, masks
Availability: health food and specialty stores in San Francisco Bay area, mail order
MO

H2O Plus, Inc.
845 W. Madison
Chicago, IL 60607
312-850-9283
800-242-BATH
Products: skin care for men and women, shaving supply, sun care, hair care, cosmetics, fragrance for men and women, baby and child care, nail care, toothbrushes, toys, toiletries
Availability: H2O Plus stores, department stores, duty-free shops, boutiques, specialty stores, mail order
MO

Huish Detergents, Inc.
3540 W. 1987 S.
P.O. Box 25057
Salt Lake City, UT 84125
801-975-3100
800-776-6702
Products: household, private-label household, all-fabric bleach
Availability: department stores, discount department stores, drugstores, supermarkets, cooperatives

Ida Grae (Nature's Colors Cosmetics)
424 La Verne Ave.
Mill Valley, CA 94941
415-388-6101
Products: cosmetics, hypoallergenic skin care for men and women, *Nature's Colors: Dyes From Plants* (book)
Availability: i natural stores, health food stores, specialty stores, boutiques, cooperatives, mail order
MO

Il-Makiage
107 E. 60th St.
New York, NY 10022
800-722-1011
Products: cosmetics, hair care, hair color, nail care, hypo-allergenic skin care for women
Availability: cooperatives, Il-Makiage stores, boutiques, specialty stores, salons, health spas, mail order
🛁 MO

Ilona Inc.
3201 E. Second Ave.
Denver, CO 80206
303-322-3000
888-38-ILONA
www.ilona.com
Products: aromatherapy, cosmetics, fragrance for women, hair care, nail care, skin care for men and women, sun care, toiletries
Availability: Ilona stores, boutiques, specialty stores, mail order
MO

Image Laboratories, Inc.
2340 Eastman Ave.
Oxnard, CA 93030
805-988-1767
800-421-8528
Products: hair care, dandruff shampoo, hair color, permanents
Availability: salons

i natural cosmetics (Cosmetic Source)
32-02 Queen's Blvd.
Long Island City, NY 11101
718-729-2929
800-962-5387
Products: cosmetics, toiletries, hair care, hypo-allergenic skin care for men and women, sun care, shaving supply
Availability: i natural stores, General Nutrition Centers
🛁

Innovative Formulations, Inc.
1810 S. Sixth Ave.
S. Tucson, AZ 85713
520-628-1553
Products: paint, coatings for roofs, household, roofing material, architectural paint, nail polish remover
Availability: mail order
V MO

41

International Rotex, Inc.
P.O. Box 20697
Reno, NV 89515
702-356-8356
800-648-1871
Products: office supply, correction fluid
Availability: discount department stores, drugstores, supermarkets, cooperatives, wholesale distributors
V

International Vitamin Corporation
209 40th St.
Irvington, NJ 07111
201-371-7300
Products: vitamins
Availability: health food stores, mail order
MO

InterNatural
P.O. Box 1008
Silver Lake, WI 53170
414-889-8501
800-548-3824
www.internatural.com
Products: aromatherapy, condoms, cosmetics, dental care, feminine hygiene, dandruff shampoo, hair color, furniture polish, laundry detergent, insect repellant, nail care, skin care, sun care, toiletries, herbs
Availability: Internet, mail order
MO

IQ Products Company
16212 State Hwy. 249
Houston, TX 77086
281-444-6454
Products: hair care, insect repellent, car care, cleaning supply
Availability: discount stores, drugstores, grocery stores

IV Trail Products
P.O. Box 1033
Sykesville, MD 21784
410-795-8989
Products: companion animal care for horses
Availability: mail order
V MO

Jacki's Magic Lotion
258 A St., #7A
Ashland, OR 97520
503-488-1388
Products: skin care for men and women, massage lotion
Availability: health food stores, massage product retailers, health spas, cooperatives, mail order
MO

James Austin Company (Austin Diversified)
P.O. Box 827
115 Downieville Rd.
Mars, PA 16046
724-625-1535
800-245-1942
Products: liquid laundry detergent, bleach, carpet cleaning supply, fabric softener, glass cleaner, ammonia, multipurpose cleaner
Availability: discount department stores, drugstores, supermarkets
Note: no catalog
MO

Jason Natural Cosmetics
8468 Warner Dr.
Culver City, CA 90232-2484
310-838-7543
800-527-6605
www.jason-natural.com
Products: aromatherapy, lubricants, feminine hygiene, hair care, dandruff shampoo, hair color, insect repellant, nail care, hypo-allergenic skin care, sun care, bathing supply, deodorant, soap
Availability: drugstores, health food stores, cooperatives, boutiques, specialty stores, mail order
★ MO

J.C. Garet, Inc.
2471 Coral St.
Vista, CA 92083
619-598-0505
800-548-9770
Products: household cleaning supply, laundry soap
Availability: department stores, supermarkets, drugstores, health food stores, cooperatives, boutiques, uniform stores, distributors
MO

Jeanne Rose Aromatherapy
219 Carl St.
San Francisco, CA 94117-3804
415-564-6785
Products: aromatherapy, companion animal care, hypo-allergenic skin care for men and women, toiletries, herbs, oil
Availability: health food stores, cooperatives, boutiques, specialty stores, independent sales representatives, mail order
MO

42

/J/Ā/S/Ö/N/®
NATURAL COSMETICS

Sold Exclusively at Your Friendly Neighborhood
Health/Natural Food Store.

*Serving Your Personal Care Needs
for 40 Years
Organic, Vegan, Pure and Natural*

1-800-JASON-05
Call ext. 302 or 314 for a FREE Catalogue...
Mention this ad and receive a FREE Sample!

http://www.jason-natural.com • E-mail: jnp@jason-natural.com
**JASON NATURAL COSMETICS Cruelty Free, Environmentally Safe —
The Best Natural and Botanical Ingredients From Around The World. Naturally, since 1959**
8468 Warner Drive • Culver City, CA 90232-2484 • Tel 310.838.7543 • Fax 310.838.9274 • ©1998

CRUELTY FREE

Jennifer Tara Cosmetics
775 E. Blithedale, #195
Mill Valley, CA 94941
800-818-8272
wfk3@earthlink.com
Products: cosmetics, skin care
Availability: mail order
★ MO

Jessica McClintock, Inc.
1400 16th St.
San Francisco, CA 94103-5181
415-495-3030
800-333-5301
Products: Jessica McClintock fragrance for women, Scott McClintock fragrance for men, toiletries, shaving supply
Availability: department stores, specialty stores, Jessica McClintock stores, boutiques, mail order
MO

Jheri Redding (Conair Corporation)
1 Cummings Point Rd.
Stamford, CT 06904
203-351-9000
800-7-CONAIR
Products: hair care, permanents, toiletries, Conair hair-care styling tools
Availability: drugstores, supermarkets, beauty supply stores, discount department stores

Joe Blasco Cosmetics
7340 Greenbriar Pkwy.
Orlando, FL 32819
407-363-7070
800-553-1520
Products: cosmetics, skin care, theatrical makeup and supply
Availability: salons, mail order
MO

John Amico Expressive Hair Care Products
4731 W. 136th St.
Crestwood, IL 60445
708-824-4000
800-676-5264
Products: hair care, dandruff shampoo, permanents, hair color, toiletries, bathing supply, soap, shaving supply
Availability: salons, mail order
MO

John Paul Mitchell Systems
9701 Wilshire Blvd.
Suite 1205
Beverly Hills, CA 90212
310-248-3888
800-321-JPMS
Products: hair care, skin care, sun care
Availability: salons
V ★

JOICO Laboratories, Inc.
P.O. Box 42308
Los Angeles, CA 90042-0308
686-968-6111
800-44-JOICO
www.joico.com
Products: hair care, hair color, permanents, skin care, toiletries, bathing supply
Availability: salons, beauty supply stores
V

Jolen Creme Bleach, Inc.
25 Walls Dr.
P.O. Box 458
Fairfield, CT 06430
203-259-8779
Products: Jolen Creme Bleach for facial and body hair
Availability: supermarkets, drugstores, discount department stores

J.R. Liggett, Ltd.
R.R. 2, Box 911
Cornish, NH 03745
603-675-2055
www.jrliggett.com
Products: hair care, dandruff shampoo
Availability: drugstores, health food stores, cooperatives, boutiques, specialty stores, independent sales representatives, mail order
V ★ MO

Jurlique Cosmetics
1000 Holcombe Woods Pkwy., Suite 318
Roswell, GA 30076
770-643-6999
800-854-1110
Products: sun care, baby care, toiletries, household, hair care, dandruff oil, cosmetics
Availability: salons, spas, mail order
MO

Katonah Scentral
51 Katonah Ave.
Katonah, NY 10536
914-232-7519
800-29-SCENT
Products: toiletries, hair care, shaving supply, fragrance for men and women, essential oil, baby care, dental hygiene, toothbrushes, hair color, aromatherapy
Availability: Katonah Scentral stores, mail order
MO

45

K.B. Products, Inc.
20 N. Railroad Ave.
San Mateo, CA 94401
415-344-6500
800-342-4321
Products: companion animal care, hair care, dandruff shampoo, hand lotion
Availability: companion animal supply stores, groomers, K.B. stores, mail order
MO

Kenic Pet Products, Inc.
109 S. Main St.
Lawrenceburg, KY 40342
800-228-7387
glomarr@igLou.com
Products: companion animal care
Availability: drugstores, health food stores, independent sales representatives, companion animal supply stores, grooming stores, hardware stores, mail order, veterinary clinics
MO

Ken Lange No-Thio Permanent Waves & Hair
7112 N. 15th Place, Suite 1
Phoenix, AZ 85020
800-486-3033
Products: hair care, permanents
Availability: salons
V

Kenra Laboratories, Inc.
6501 Julian Ave.
Indianapolis, IN 46219
317-356-6491
800-428-8073
Products: hair care, skin care
Availability: salons

Kiehl's Since 1851
109 Third Ave.
New York, NY 10003
973-244-9828
800-KIEHLS1
Products: baby care, cosmetics, fragrance for men and women, hair care, skin care, sun care
Availability: department stores, mail order, Kiehl's stores
MO

Kimberly Sayer, Inc.
125 W. 81st St., #2A
New York, NY 10024
212-362-2907
Products: hypo-allergenic skin care for men and women, toiletries
Availability: distributors, boutiques, specialty stores, mail order
MO

Kiss My Face
P.O. Box 224
144 Main St.
Gardiner, NY 12525
914-255-0884
800-262-KISS
www.kissmyface.com
Products: hair care, skin care for men and women, sun care, cosmetics, toiletries, shaving supply, baby care
Availability: health food stores, drugstores, cooperatives, boutiques, massage therapists, salons, mail order
★ MO

Kleen Brite Laboratories, Inc.
200 State St.
Brockport, NY 14420
716-637-0630
800-223-1473
Products: household, bleach, laundry detergents
Availability: drugstores, supermarkets

KMS Research, Inc.
4712 Mountain Lakes Blvd.
Redding, CA 96003
916-244-6000
800-DIAL-KMS
www.kmshaircare.com
Products: hair care, dandruff shampoo, permanents
Availability: salons

KSA Jojoba
19025 Parthenia St., #200
Northridge, CA 91324
818-701-1534
jojoba99@hotmail.com
Products: baby care, companion animal care, cosmetics, fragrance, hair care, skin care, toiletries, bathing supply, soap
Availability: mail order
V ★ MO

La Costa Products International
2875 Loker Ave. E.
Carlsbad, CA 92008
619-438-2181
800-LA-COSTA
Products: cosmetics, hair care, nail care, skin care for women, sun care, shaving supply, toiletries
Availability: salons, mail order
MO

Legend

V Vegan (products contain no animal ingredients)

★ Company meets CSCA

▨ Company uses Caring Consumer product logo

MO Mail order available

Cleanse • Tone • Moisturize
with LaCrista Natural Skin Care Products

| Tropical Body Soap | Oatmeal Scrub | Hydrating Toner | Dewberry Lotion | Almond Oil Moisturizer | Variety of Tote Bags & Aromatherapy Candles |

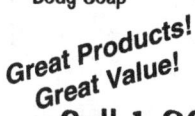

La Crista
The Skin Care Specialist ... Naturally

Great Products! Great Value!

NOT TESTED ON ANIMALS
Never Have, Never Will!

Call 1-800-888-2231 for more information
or E-mail us at Skincare@LaCrista.com

Natural • No Mineral Oil or Harsh Chemicals • Affordably Priced
Available at Giant Food & Pharmacy Stores, U.S. Commissaries-Worldwide, The Cosmetic Center, Fresh Fields, and many independent health food and drug stores
(See our coupon for free trial-size Dewberry Lotion!)

La Crista, Inc.
P.O. Box 240
Davisonville, MD 21035
410-956-4447
800-888-2231
skincare@LaCrista.com
Products: aromatherapy, baby care, cosmetics, massage oil, hypo-allergenic skin care for men and women, bathing supply, soap
Availability: discount department stores, health food stores, supermarkets, commissary, Wal-mart, mail order
V ✈ MO

Lady of the Lake
P.O. Box 7140
Brookings, OR 97415
541-469-3354
Products: aromatherapy, homeopathic remedies, water treatment systems, books
Availability: Lady of the Lake Store, mail order
★ MO

LaNatura
425 N. Bedford Dr.
Beverly Hills, CA 90210
310-271-5616
800-352-6288
Products: baby care, cosmetics, fragrance for women, skin care, toiletries, bathing supply, soap
Availability: health food stores, LaNatura stores, boutiques, specialty stores, hotel private label, mail order
V MO

Lancôme
575 Fifth Ave.
New York, NY 10017
212-818-1500
Products: cosmetics, sun care
Availability: department stores
Note: Lancôme does not test its products on animals. It may, however, test its ingredients on animals.

Lander Company, Inc.
106 Grand Ave.
Englewood, NJ 07631
201-568-9700
800-4-LANDER
www.lander-hgc.com
Products: aromatherapy, baby care, dental hygiene, hair care, dandruff shampoo, skin care, toiletries, bathing supply, deodorant, shaving supply, soap
Availability: drugstores, supermarkets

47

From nature without cruelty.

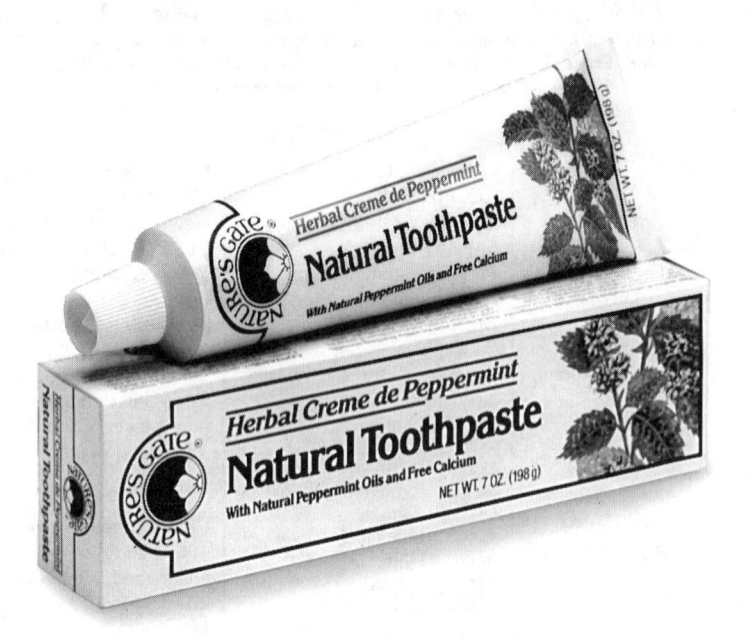

L'anza Research International, Inc.
935 W. Eighth St.
Azusa, CA 91702
818-334-9333
800-423-0307
Products: hair care, dandruff shampoo, permanents, hair color
Availability: salons
V

La Prairie, Inc.
31 W. 52nd St.
New York, NY 10019
212-459-1600
800-821-5718
Products: cosmetics, fragrance for men and women, skin care for women, sun care
Availability: department stores, boutiques, specialty stores

Lee Pharmaceuticals
1434 Santa Anita Ave.
S. El Monte, CA 91733
818-442-3141
800-950-5337
Products: Lee acrylic nails and nail care, Nose Better, Zip hair removal, Saxon aftershave cream, Sundance aloe, Peterson's ointment, Creamalin antacid, Bikini Bare depilatory
Availability: drugstores, grocery stores, boutiques

Legend
V Vegan (products contain no animal ingredients)
★ Company meets CSCA
🖐 Company uses Caring Consumer product logo
MO Mail order available

Levlad/Nature's Gate Herbal Cosmetics
9200 Mason Ave.
Chatsworth, CA 91311
818-882-2951
800-327-2012
www.levlad.com
Products: dental hygiene, toiletries, sun care, hypo-allergenic skin care for women, dandruff shampoo, soap, deodorant, bathing supply
Availability: health food stores, drugstores, cooperatives, supermarkets, mail order
★ MO

Liberty Natural Products, Inc.
8120 S.E. Stock St.
Portland, OR 97215
503-256-1227
800-289-8427
Products: baby care, air freshener, dental hygiene, sun care, toothbrushes, toiletries, fragrance for women, skin care, household
Availability: health food stores, cooperatives
V

Life Dynamics, Inc.
21640 N. 19th Ave.
Suite C101
Phoenix, AZ 85027
602-582-5977
800-977-9664
Products: hair care, hypo-allergenic skin care for men and women, toiletries, natural color protection
Availability: distributors, specialty stores, mail order
MO

Life Tree Products
P.O. Box 1203
Sebastopol, CA 95473
707-588-0755
Products: household, dishwashing detergent, laundry detergent, all-purpose cleaning supply, liquid soap
Availability: drugstores, health food stores, supermarkets, cooperatives, mail order
V MO

Lightning Products
1900 Erie St.
N. Kansas City, MO 64116
816-221-3183
Products: companion animal care, household, carpet cleaning supply
Availability: companion animal supply stores, health food stores, mail order
MO

Lily of Colorado
P.O. Box 12471
Denver, CO 80212
303-455-4194
Products: purely botanical skin care
Availability: health food stores, mail order
MO

Lime-O-Sol Company (The Works)
P.O. Box 395
Ashley, IN 46705
219-587-9151
Products: household cleaning supply, drain opener
Availability: department stores, discount department stores, drugstores, supermarkets

49

Lissée Cosmetics
927 McGarry St.
Los Angeles, CA 90021
213-488-0777
Products: cosmetics, aromatherapy, skin care for women, hair care, dandruff shampoo, sun care
Availability: drugstores, beauty supply stores, boutiques, specialty stores
V

Little Forest Natural Baby Products, Inc.
2415 Third St., Suite #270
San Francisco, CA 94107
415-621-6504
dosburn@littleforest.com
Products: baby care
Availability: health food stores, baby boutiques
V **★**

Liz Claiborne Cosmetics, Inc.
1441 Broadway
New York, NY 10018
212-354-4900
Products: fragrance, toiletries, shaving supply, bathing supply, deodorant, soap
Availability: department stores, Liz Claiborne stores

Lobob Laboratories
1440 Atteberry La.
San Jose, CA 95131-1410
408-432-0580
800-83LOBOB
loblabs@aol.com
Products: hard and soft contact lens cleaner, wetting solution, soaking solution
Availability: mail order, grocery stores, drugstores
V **★** **MO**

Logona USA, Inc.
554-E Riverside Dr.
Asheville, NC 28801
704-252-1420
Products: hair care, baby care, dental hygiene, hypo-allergenic skin care for men and women, hair color, sun care, fragrance for men, toiletries, shaving supply, dandruff shampoo
Availability: health food stores, cooperatives, boutiques, specialty stores, mail order
MO

L'Oréal (Cosmair)
575 Fifth Ave.
New York, NY 10017
212-818-1500
www.lorealcosmetics.com
Products: cosmetics, hair care, fragrance for men and women, hair color, nail care, permanents, hypo-allergenic skin care for men and women, toiletries
Availability: department stores, drugstores, supermarkets, boutiques, specialty stores, discount department stores
Note: L'Oréal does not test its products on animals. It may, however, test its ingredients on animals.

Lotus Light
1100 Lotus Dr.
Silver Lake, WI 53170
414-889-8501
800-548-3824
Products: aromatherapy, baby care, companion animal care, condoms, lubricants, cosmetics, dental hygiene, toothbrushes, feminine hygiene, fragrance, hair care, insect repellant, skin care, toiletries, soap, vitamins, herbs
Availability: drugstores, health food stores, cooperatives, mail order
MO

Louise Bianco Skin Care, Inc.
13655 Chandler Blvd.
Sherman Oaks, CA 91401
818-786-2700
800-782-3067
www.louisebianco.com
Products: hypo-allergenic skin care for men and women, sun care, toiletries, bathing supply, deodorant, soap
Availability: mail order, salons
MO

M.A.C. Cosmetics
233 Carlton St., Suite 201
Toronto, ON M5A 2L2
Canada
416-924-0598
800-387-6707
Products: cosmetics, hypo-allergenic skin care for men and women, nail care, hair care, theatrical makeup
Availability: department stores, M.A.C. Cosmetics stores

Legend

V Vegan (products contain no animal ingredients)

★ Company meets CSCA

▨ Company uses Caring Consumer product logo

MO Mail order available

Magick Botanicals
3412 W. MacArthur Blvd., #K
Santa Ana, CA 92704
714-957-0674
800-237-0674
Products: hair care, skin care for men and women, toiletries, baby care
Availability: health food stores, mail order
MO

Magic of Aloe
7300 N. Crescent Blvd.
Pennsauken, NJ 08110
609-662-3334
800-257-7770
Products: cosmetics, hair care, skin care for men and women, sun care, toiletries, shaving supply
Availability: health food stores, boutiques, specialty stores, Value Vision Home Shopping, distributors, mail order
MO

Mallory Pet Supplies
118 Atrisco Dr. S.W.
Albuquerque, NM 87105
505-836-4033
800-824-4464
Products: companion animal care
Availability: companion animal supply stores, mail order
MO

Marcal Paper Mills, Inc.
1 Market St.
Elmwood Park, NJ 07407
201-796-4000
www.marcalpaper.com
Products: household paper, toilet paper
Availability: supermarkets, drugstores
V

Marché Image Corporation
P.O. Box 1010
Bronxville, NY 10708
914-793-2093
800-753-9980
cmarch4416@aol.com
Products: skin care for men and women, tanning cream, household, carpet cleaning supply
Availability: distributors, mail order
MO

Marilyn Miglin Institute
112 E. Oak St.
Chicago, IL 60611
312-943-1120
800-662-1120
Products: skin care, cosmetics, fragrance for men and women
Availability: Marilyn Miglin Institute, sales consultants, mail order
MO

Masada Marketing Company
P.O. Box 4118
Chatsworth, CA 91313
818-717-8300
800-368-8811
www.masada-spa.com
Products: Dead Sea mineral bath salts
Availability: health food stores, cooperatives, mail order
V MO

Mastey de Paris, Inc.
25413 Rye Canyon Rd.
Valencia, CA 91355
805-257-4814
800-6-MASTEY
Products: hair care, sun care, hair color, toiletries, skin care, permanents, dandruff shampoo
Availability: salons, beauty schools, mail order
MO

Maybelline, Inc.
P.O. Box 372
Memphis, TN 38101-0372
901-324-0310
800-944-0730
Products: cosmetics
Availability: grocery stores, drugstores
Note: Maybelline was purchased by L'Oréal in 1996. It does not test its products or ingredients on animals.

Mehron, Inc.
100 Red Schoolhouse Rd.
Chestnut Ridge, NY 10977
914-426-1700
800-332-9955
sale@mehron.com
Products: theatrical makeup, cosmetics
Availability: boutiques, specialty stores, party supply and costume stores, mail order
MO

Mère Cie, Inc.
1100 Soscol Ferry Rd., #3
Napa, CA 94558
707-257-8510
800-832-4544
merecie@merecie.com
Products: aromatherapy, fragrance for men and women, household, air freshener
Availability: department stores, drugstores, health food stores, supermarkets, cooperatives, boutiques, specialty stores, mail order
MO

Merle Norman
9130 Bellanca Ave.
Los Angeles, CA 90045
310-641-3000
www.merlenorman.com
Products: cosmetics, skin care
Availability: Merle Norman salons

Mia Rose Products, Inc.
177-F Riverside Ave.
Newport Beach, CA 92663
714-662-5465
800-292-6339
www.miarose.com
Products: household, aromatherapy
Availability: health food stores, boutiques, cooperatives, drugstores, specialty stores, mail order, supermarkets, distributors
V ★ 🖎 MO

Michael's Naturopathic Programs
6203 Woodlake Center
San Antonio, TX 78244
210-661-8311
800-525-9643
www.michaelshealth.com
Products: vitamins, herbs
Availability: health food stores
★

Michelle Lazar Cosmetics
755 S. Lugo Ave.
San Bernardino, CA 92048
909-888-6310
Products: skin care
Availability: health food stores, mail order
MO

Micro Balanced Products
20 Foster St.
P.O. Box 8
Bergenfield, NJ 07621
201-387-0200
800-626-7888
Products: hypo-allergenic skin care for men and women, sun care, toiletries
Availability: health food stores, mail order
V MO

Mill Creek Botanicals
620 Airpark Rd.
Napa, CA 94558
800-447-6758
www.millcreekbotanicals.com
Products: hair care, dandruff shampoo, skin care for women, sun care, toiletries, bathing supply, deodorant, shaving supply, soap, vitamins, herbs
Availability: drugstores, health food stores, supermarkets

Mira Linder Spa in the City
29935 Northwestern Hwy.
Southfield, MI 48034
800-321-8860
Products: cosmetics, hypo-allergenic skin care for men and women, nail care
Availability: Mira Linder Spa in the City stores, mail order
MO

Legend

V	Vegan (products contain no animal ingredients)
★	Company meets CSCA
🖎	Company uses Caring Consumer product logo
MO	Mail order available

Montagne Jeunesse
Eco-Factory, Off Valley Way
Llansamlet, Swansea
SA6 8QP Wales
Great Britain
01792-310306
Products: aromatherapy, hair care, nail care, skin care for women, toiletries, bathing supply, soap
Availability: department stores, discount department stores, drugstores, health food stores, supermarkets, cooperatives, boutiques, specialty stores, independent sales representatives
★

Mother's Little Miracle, Inc.
27520 Hawthorne Blvd.
Suite 125
Rolling Hills Estates, CA 90274
310-544-7125
Products: baby care, children's stain and odor remover and prewash, spit-up remover, air freshener
Availability: drugstores, discount department stores, boutiques, specialty stores, distributors, mail order
V MO

Mountain Ocean Ltd.
5150 Valmont Rd.
Boulder, CO 80306
303-444-2781
Products: baby care (prenatal), hair care, toiletries
Availability: health food stores, supermarkets, mail order
MO

Mr. Christal's
10877 Wilshire Blvd.
12th Fl.
Los Angeles, CA 90024
310-824-2508
800-426-0108
www.mrchristals.com
Products: companion animal care
Availability: companion animal supply stores, veterinarians

Nadina's Cremes
3600 Clipper Mill Rd.
Suite 140
Baltimore, MD 21211
410-235-9192
800-722-4292
Products: scented body cream for men and women, body care
Availability: health food stores, drugstores, cooperatives, boutiques, specialty stores, independent sales representatives, environmental stores, New Age stores, mail order
★ MO

Nala Barry Labs
P.O. Box 151
Palm Desert, CA 92261
619-321-7098
800-397-4174
Products: companion animal care, nutritional supplements
Availability: health food stores, cooperatives, boutiques, garden shops, companion animal supply stores, specialty stores
V 🐾 MO

Narwhale of High Tor, Ltd.
591 S. Mountain Rd.
New City, NY 10956
914-634-8832
800-MD-CREAM
Products: cosmetics, hypoallergenic skin care for men and women, sun care
Availability: skin care clinics, physicians, mail order
MO

Natracare
191 University Blvd.
Suite 294
Denver, CO 80206
303-320-1510
Products: feminine hygiene
Availability: drugstores, health food stores, cooperatives, boutiques, specialty stores, mail order
V MO

Natura
27134-A Paseo Espada
Suite 323
San Juan Capestrano, CA 92675
949-240-1104
800-933-1008
Products: fragrance for men and women, aromatherapy oil, hair oil, air freshener, skin care for men and women, aromatherapy diffusers, essential oil, massage oil
Availability: health food stores, distributors, health spas, boutiques, specialty stores, aromatherapists
V 🐾 MO

Naturade Cosmetics
7110 E. Jackson St.
Paramount, CA 90723
310-531-8120
800-421-1830
www.naturade.com
Products: hair care, hypoallergenic skin care for men and women, dandruff shampoo, toiletries, baby care, companion animal care, cosmetics
Availability: health food stores, cooperatives, supermarkets, boutiques, specialty stores, mail order
🐾 MO

Natural (Surrey)
13110 Trails End Rd.
Leander, TX 78641
512-267-7172
Products: toiletries, shaving supply, soap
Availability: health food stores, drugstores, department stores, supermarkets, mail order
MO

Natural Animal Health Products, Inc.
7000 U.S. 1 N.
St. Augustine, FL 32095
904-824-5884
800-274-7387
Products: skin care for animals, Earth-safe household and yard supply
Availability: health food stores, lawn and garden stores, cooperatives, companion animal supply stores, veterinarians, groomers

Natural Bodycare, Inc.
355 N. Lantana St.
Camarillo, CA 93010
805-445-9237
Products: aromatherapy, hair care, toiletries, skin care, fragrance for women, sun care, dandruff shampoo, household
Availability: health food stores, mail order
V MO

Natural Chemistry, Inc.
76 Progress Dr.
Stamford, CT 06902
203-316-4479
800-753-1233
Products: pool supply, household, companion animal care
Availability: health food stores, cooperatives, environmental product stores, mail order
MO

Naturally Yours, Alex
1848 Murray Ave.
Clearwater, FL 33755
813-443-7479
Products: companion animal care
Availability: health food stores, companion animal supply stores, mail order, holistic veterinarians
V MO

Natural Products Company
7782 Newburg Rd.
Newburg, PA 17240-9601
717-423-5818
800-323-0418
Products: companion animal care
Availability: health food stores, gift stores, companion animal supply stores
V

Natural Research People, Inc.
South Route, Box 12
Lavina, MT 59046
406-575-4343
Products: companion animal care
Availability: health food stores, veterinarians, companion animal supply stores, cooperatives, mail order
V MO

Natural Science
Historic Graybor Bldg.
420 Lexington Ave., Suite 2104
New York, NY 10170
212-953-5200
888-EARTHSAFE
Products: fragrance for men and women, hypo-allergenic skin care for men and women, aromatherapy, baby care, cosmetics, sun care
Availability: health food stores, department stores, drugstores, mail order
V ★ MO

Natural World, Inc.
6929 E. Greenway Pkwy.
Suite 100
Scottsdale, AZ 85254
602-905-1110
800-728-3388
Products: aromatherapy, dental hygiene, hair care, household, air freshener, car care, carpet cleaning supply, furniture polish, laundry detergent, hypo-allergenic skin care, sun care, toiletries, vitamins, herbs
Availability: independent sales representatives, mail order
MO

Nature Clean (Frank T. Ross & Sons, Ltd.)
6550 Lawrence Ave. E.
Scarborough, ON M1C 4A7
Canada
416-282-1107
Products: hair care, household, bleach, car care, carpet cleaning supply, laundry detergent, glue, soap
Availability: department stores, drugstores, health food stores, supermarkets, cooperatives
V MO

Nature de France, Ltd. (Para Laboratories)
100 Rose Ave.
Hempstead, NY 11550
516-538-4600
800-645-3752
Products: ethnic products, hair care, skin care, toiletries, bathing supply, deodorant, shaving supply, soap
Availability: department stores, discount department stores, drugstores, health food stores, supermarkets, cooperatives, mail order
V MO

Nature's Acres
8984 E. Weinke Rd.
North Freedom, WI 53951
608-522-4492
Products: cosmetics, soap, toner, body oil
Availability: health food stores, mail order
MO

THEY CLEAN NATURALLY.

"My Folks Love Me..."

Each year, over 1 million accidental poisoning occur in North America. Most happen to children and are caused by toxic cleaning products.

Our non-toxic, hypoallergenic alternatives are safe enough even for those who suffer from chemical sensitivities or environmental allergies!

Look for our newest products!

Non-Toxic Oven Cleaner
Hypoallergenic Carpet Cleaner
Laundry Stain Remover
Non-Chlorine Laundry Bleach Powder
Delicate Wash for fine fabrics

NATURE CLEAN®

Truly Natural Laundry & Household Cleaning Products
A Canadian Tradition for over 30 Years

Non-Toxic ❖ Hypoallergenic ❖ Cruelty Free ❖ Fully Biodegradable ❖ Septic Safe

Available at Health Food, Bulk Foods or independant Grocery Stores or call Frank T.Ross at 416-282-1107

Nature's Best (Natural Research People)
South Route, Box 12
Lavina, MT 59046
406-575-4343
Products: companion animal care
Availability: companion animal supply stores, health food stores, mail order
V MO

Nature's Country Pet
1765 Garnet Ave., Suite 12
San Diego, CA 92109
619-230-1058
800-576-PAWS
Products: companion animal care
Availability: health food stores, companion animal supply stores; mail order
V MO

Nature's Plus
548 Broadhollow Rd.
Melville, NY 11747-3508
516-293-0030
800-645-9500
Products: dietary supplements, Nature's Plus brand, companion animal care, hair care, dandruff shampoo, nail care, skin care for men and women, toiletries, cosmetics
Availability: health food stores

Nectarine
1200 Fifth St.
Berkeley, CA 94710
510-528-0162
Products: fragrance, hair care, skin care, toiletries, bathing supply, shaving supply, soap
Availability: health food stores, boutiques, specialty stores

Neocare Laboratories, Inc.
33 Journey, Suite 200
Aliso Viejo, CA 92656
714-360-1193
Products: hypo-allergenic skin care for men and women, household, pool and spa supply, odor eliminator, grease trap and septic tank control supply
Availability: health food stores, cooperatives, mail order
V MO

New Age Products
16200 N. Hwy. 101
Willits, CA 95490-9710
707-459-5969
Products: household
Availability: health food stores
V

55

FREE THE ANIMALS!
by Ingrid Newkirk

The voice that speaks for the animals speaks for the ALF (Animal Liberation Front). At long last, the story of the ALF in America is told, by PETA cofounder Ingrid Newkirk. Scintillating details about animals rescued from testing laboratories, fur farms, and food factories make for fast-moving adventure and riveting reading. Ingrid's interviews with the stop-at-nothing, dedicated ALF leader "Valerie" and her 10-year struggle to revolutionize society's attitudes toward animals provide a behind-the-scenes look at the ALF that surpasses everything you've ever heard in the media about this shadowy group.

256 pages, paperback
Item No. BK601 $10.00

SAVE THE ANIMALS! 101 EASY THINGS YOU CAN DO
by Ingrid Newkirk

"Even the opposition must recognize an unusually fair and clear-minded spirit in Ms. Newkirk. If we all follow her reasonable, well-considered suggestions, we will soon rectify the horrible wrongs and see the end of cruelty to our fellow creatures."
Rue McClanahan

208 pages, paperback
Item No. BK590 $4.95

KIDS CAN SAVE THE ANIMALS! 101 EASY THINGS TO DO
by Ingrid Newkirk

All over the world, our animal friends are in trouble. That's the bad news. The good news is that kids can make a difference. Here is a book full of fascinating facts about animals, wonderful, whimsical drawings, and more than 100 projects and ideas that show how kids can help. Ages 8-13.

234 pages, paperback
Item No. BK205 $6.99

These books were created for those people who care enough about their fellow earthlings to do something for them. It has never been so easy, or so important, to make a difference. Read, digest, share, and act! Proceeds from the sale of these publications support PETA'S programs in behalf of animals.
Ingrid E. Newkirk

To order, write: PETA Merchandise, 501 Front St., Norfolk, VA 23510, or call 1-800-483-4366 (orders only, please) between 9:00 a.m. and 5:00 p.m. EST, Monday through Friday.

Neway
Little Harbor
42 Doaks La.
Marblehead, MA 01945
617-631-9400
Products: household
Availability: health food stores, mail order
V MO

Neways, Inc.
150 E. 400 N.
Salem, UT 84653
801-423-2800
800-998-7233
Products: cosmetics, hair care, hypo-allergenic skin care for men and women, sun care, toiletries, shaving supply, dental hygiene, household, nail care
Availability: distributors, boutiques, specialty stores, mail order
MO

New Chapter Extracts, Inc.
99 Main St.
P.O. Box 1947
Brattleboro, VT 05301
802-257-0018
800-543-7279
www.newchapter.com
Products: skin care, nutritional supplements, herbal extracts, ginger delivery system
Availability: health food stores, cooperatives, physicians, estheticians, mail order
V MO

Nexxus Products Company
82 Coromar Dr.
Santa Barbara, CA 93111
805-968-6900
www.nexxusproducts.com
Products: hair color, hair care, permanents, vitamins, toiletries, dandruff shampoo
Availability: salons

Nirvana, Inc.
P.O. Box 26275
Minneapolis, MN 55426
612-932-2919
800-432-2919
Products: aromatherapy, hair care, skin care
Availability: drugstores, health food stores, cooperatives, mail order
V ★ MO

No Common Scents
Kings Yard
220 Xenia Ave.
Yellow Springs, OH 45387
937-767-4261
800-686-0012
Products: fragrance for men and women, air freshener, companion animal care, incense, bath crystals
Availability: No Common Scents store, mail order
MO

Nordstrom
865 Market St.
San Francisco, CA 94103
800-7-BEAUTY
Products: Nordstrom Bath Ltd. (bathing supply), Simple and Natural Essentials (skin care and makeup), Nordstrom Essentials (bathing supply), Single Notes (fragrance)
Availability: Nordstrom department stores, mail order
MO

Norelco
1010 Washington Blvd.
P.O. Box 120015
Stamford, CT 06912-0015
203-973-0200
Products: electric razors
Availability: department stores, drugstores, supermarkets
V

North Country Soap
7888 County Rd., #6
Maple Plain, MN 55359
612-479-3381
800-667-1202
Products: baby care, companion animal care, insect repellant, hypo-allergenic skin care, sun care, toiletries, bathing supply, deodorant, soap
Availability: drugstores, health food stores, North Country Soap stores, boutiques, specialty stores, independent sales representatives, mail order, museum gift shops, resorts, hotels, sports shops
MO

N/R Laboratories, Inc.
900 E. Franklin St.
Centerville, OH 45459
513-433-9570
800-223-9348
Products: companion animal care
Availability: distributors, mail order
MO

NuSkin International, Inc.
One NuSkin Plaza
75 W. Center
Provo, UT 84601
801-377-6056
800-366-6875
www.nuskin.com
Products: hair care, skin care for men and women, sun care, toiletries, nutritional supplements
Availability: distributors, mail order
MO

57

NutriBiotic
865 Parallel Dr.
Lakeport, CA 95453
707-263-0411
800-225-4345
Products: dental hygiene, nutritional supplements, toiletries
Availability: health food stores

Nutri-Cell, Inc. (Derma-Glo)
1038 N. Tustin, Suite 309
Orange, CA 92667-5958
714-953-8307
Products: companion animal care, hypo-allergenic skin care for men and women, sun care
Availability: health food stores, drugstores, supermarkets, cooperatives, mail order
[V] [MO]

Nutri-Metics International, USA, Inc.
12723 E. 166th St.
Cerritos, CA 90703
562-802-0411
800-267-7546
Products: cosmetics, toiletries, household
Availability: distributors, mail order
[MO]

Nutrina Company, Inc.
1727 Cosmic Way
Glendale, CA 91201
818-790-1776
800-523-8899
Products: vitamins, herbs
Availability: health food stores, cooperatives, mail order
[MO]

Ohio Hempery, Inc.
7002 S.R. 329
Guysville, OH 45735
614-662-4367
800-BUY-HEMP
www.hempery.com
Products: cosmetics, skin care, clothing, hemp
Availability: health food stores, mail order
[MO]

Oliva Ltd.
P.O. Box 4387
Reading, PA 19606
610-779-7854
Products: toiletries, soap
Availability: health food stores, cooperatives, mail order
[V] [MO]

OPI Products, Inc.
13034 Saticoy St.
N. Hollywood, CA 91605
818-759-2400
800-341-9999
opinails@aol.com
Products: nail care
Availability: beauty salons, professional beauty supply stores

Orange-Mate
P.O. Box 883
Waldport, OR 97394
503-563-3290
800-626-8685
Products: air freshener
Availability: department stores, discount department stores, drugstores, health food stores, cooperatives, specialty stores, independent sales representatives
[V] [MO]

Oriflame Corporation
4434 Cerritos Ave.
Las Alamitos, CA 90720
714-229-1160
800-959-0699
Products: toiletries, hypo-allergenic skin care for men and women, sun care, cosmetics, fragrance for men and women, hair care, vitamins
Availability: distributors, mail order
[MO]

Origins Natural Resources (Estée Lauder)
767 Fifth Ave.
New York, NY 10153
212-572-4100
Products: sensory therapy, cosmetics, skin care, fragrance, sun care, toiletries, bathing supply, soap, shaving supply, vegan makeup brushes
Availability: department stores, Origins stores, boutiques, specialty stores

Orjene Natural Cosmetics
5-43 48th Ave.
Long Island City, NY 11101
718-937-2666
800-886-7536
Products: cosmetics, toiletries, shaving supply, skin care for men and women, sun care, hair care
Availability: health food stores, cooperatives, mail order
[MO]

Orlane
555 Madison Ave.
New York, NY 10022
212-750-1111
800-535-3628
Products: cosmetics, fragrance for women, nail care, hypo-allergenic skin care for women, sun care
Availability: department stores, boutiques, specialty stores, distributors

Orly International, Inc.
9309 Deering Ave.
Chatsworth, CA 91311
818-998-1111
800-275-1111
Products: cosmetics, nail care, skin care for women
Availability: drugstores, supermarkets, salons, beauty supply stores

Otto Basics—Beauty 2 Go!
P.O. Box 9023
Rancho Santa Fe, CA 92067
619-756-2026
800-598-OTTO
Products: cosmetics
Availability: department stores, QVC television, direct TV marketing
MO

Oxyfresh Worldwide, Inc.
E. 12928 Indiana Ave.
P.O. Box 3723
Spokane, WA 99220
509-924-4999
Products: companion animal care, dental hygiene, toothbrushes, hair care, household, air freshener, laundry detergent, skin care for men and women, toiletries, bathing supply, soap, vitamins, herbs
Availability: independent sales representatives, mail order
V MO

Pacific Scents, Inc.
P.O. Box 8205
Calabasas, CA 91375-8205
818-999-0832
800-554-7236
Products: essential oil, toiletries, audiocassettes with subliminal affirmations
Availability: health food stores, mail order
V MO

Parfums Houbigant Paris
1135 Pleasant View Terr. W.
Ridgefield, NJ 07657
Products: fragrance for men and women, toiletries, skin care for men and women
Availability: department stores, boutiques, specialty stores, mail order
MO

Parlux Fragrances, Inc.
3725 S.W. 30th Ave.
Ft. Lauderdale, FL 33312
954-316-9008
800-727-5895
Products: cosmetics, fragrance for men and women
Availability: department stores, boutiques, specialty stores, drugstores
V

Pathmark Stores, Inc.
301 Blair Rd.
Woodbridge, NJ 07095
908-499-3000
Products: dental hygiene, toothbrushes, baking soda, razors, vitamins, air freshener
Availability: Pathmark supermarkets and drugstores

Patricia Allison Natural Beauty Products
4470 Monahan Rd.
La Mesa, CA 91941
619-444-4163
800-858-8742
Products: cosmetics, fragrance for women, skin care for men and women, hypo-allergenic, sun care, toiletries, bathing supply, massage oil
Availability: mail order
MO

Paul Mazzotta, Inc.
P.O. Box 96
Reading, PA 19607
610-376-2250
800-562-1357
Products: cosmetics, hair care, dandruff shampoo, hair color, permanents, hypo-allergenic skin care for men and women, sun care, toiletries
Availability: salons, Paul Mazzotta stores
V 🏠 MO

Paul Mitchell
9701 Wilshire Blvd.
Suite 1205
Beverly Hills, CA 90212
310-248-3888
800-321-JPMS
Products: hair care, skin care, sun care
Availability: salons
V ★

Legend

V Vegan (products contain no animal ingredients)

★ Company meets CSCA

🏠 Company uses Caring Consumer product logo

MO Mail order available

Paul Penders Company, Inc.
1340 Commerce St.
Petaluma, CA 94954
707-763-5828
800-440-7285
Products: cosmetics, hair care, hair color, hypo-allergenic skin care, toiletries, bathing supply, shaving supply
Availability: health food stores, mail order
MO

Perfect Balance Cosmetics, Inc.
2 Ridgewood Rd.
Malvern, PA 19355-9629
610-647-7780
Products: thigh-smoothing cream, cosmetics, hypo-allergenic skin care for men and women, hair care, fragrance for men and women, sun care
Availability: distributors, salons, health spas and clubs, independent sales representatives, mail order
MO

The Pet Connection
P.O. Box 391806
Mountain View, CA 94039
650-949-1190
Products: companion animal care, carpet cleaning supply
Availability: companion animal supply stores, mail order, department stores, drugstores, health food stores, cooperatives
MO

PetGuard, Inc.
165 Industrial Loop S.
Unit 5
Orange Park, FL 32073
904-264-8500
800-874-3221
Products: companion animal care
Availability: health food stores, companion animal supply stores, veterinary offices, environmental product stores, cooperatives

Pets 'n People, Inc. (Nature's Miracle)
27520 Hawthorne Blvd.
Suite 215
Rolling Hills Estates, CA 90274
310-544-7125
Products: Nature's Miracle, companion animal cleaning supply, litter treatment, carpet cleaning supply
Availability: companion animal supply stores, distributors, mail order
V MO

Pharmagel International
P.O. Box 2288
Monterey, CA 93942
408-649-2300
800-882-4889
Products: hypo-allergenic skin care for men and women, sun care, bathing supply, shaving supply, soap
Availability: health food stores, boutiques, specialty stores, mail order, salons
V MO

Pilot Corporation of America
60 Commerce Dr.
Trumbull, CT 06611
203-377-8800
www.pilotpen.com
Products: office supply, writing instruments
Availability: office supply stores, grocery stores, drugstores, catalogs
V

Planet, Inc.
P.O. Box 48184
Victoria, BC V8Z 7H6
Canada
800-858-8449
www.planetinc.com
Products: household, all-purpose cleaner, dishwashing liquid, laundry detergent
Availability: health food stores, supermarkets, cooperatives, mail order
V MO

PlantEssence Natural Body Care
P.O. Box 14743
Portland, OR 97293-0743
503-281-4147
800-752-6898
Products: air freshener, body oil, lip balm, fragrance for men and women, toiletries, skin care for men and women, mouth freshener
Availability: health food stores, cooperatives, boutiques, specialty stores, mail order
MO

Compassionate Cooks Use THE COMPASSIONATE COOK

A VEGETARIAN COOKBOOK BY PEOPLE FOR THE ETHICAL TREATMENT OF ANIMALS AND INGRID NEWKIRK

Millions of Americans are making the switch to compassionate food choices—for the animals, for their health, and for a healthier planet. For all you compassionate cooks, or for those you would like to introduce to vegetarianism, we've compiled the favorite recipes of PETA staff and members—including k.d. lang's Indonesian Salad with Spicy Peanut Dressing, Linda McCartney's Avocado and Green Chili Soup, and Kevin Nealon's Delicious and Simple Chili. Here is a book filled with wonderful recipes that make vegan cooking fun and easy. From soup to nuts, burgers to holiday meals, breakfast to dessert, this cookbook has the recipes you're looking for, whether you're a beginner or an experienced cook.

Happy—and compassionate—eating!

"LEAVE IT TO PETA TO PUBLISH A BOOK FULL OF ANSWERS FOR THOSE WHO WANT TO EAT CONSCIOUSLY AND WELL."
— Alec Baldwin

"PETA'S COOKBOOK IS THE BEST WAY I KNOW FOR PEOPLE TO SHOW THAT THEY CARE ABOUT ANIMALS. I USE IT EVERY DAY I'M HOME!"
— Rue McClanahan

"INGRID'S BOOK OFFERS DELICIOUS, HEALTHY VEGAN RECIPES FOR THOSE OF US WHO LOVE ANIMALS AND LOVE TO EAT...LIKE ME! A MUST FOR THE EXPERIENCED VEGETARIAN AND THOSE TRYING TO KICK THE MEAT HABIT!"
— Kevin Nealon

PeTA TO ORDER, SEND A $15 CHECK OR MONEY ORDER (POSTAGE INCLUDED) TO:
PETA MERCHANDISE • 501 Front St., Norfolk, VA 23510

Potions & Lotions—Body and Soul, Inc.
10201 N. 21st Ave., #8
Phoenix, AZ 85021
602-944-6642
800-456-3765
Products: aromatherapy, fragrance for men and women, hair care, sun care, hypo-allergenic skin care for men and women, shaving supply, air freshener, toothbrushes, toiletries, baby care
Availability: health food stores, boutiques, specialty stores, Potions & Lotions stores, mail order
🏠 MO

Prescription Plus Clinical Skin Care
25028 Kearny Ave.
Valencia, CA 91355
800-877-4849
Products: skin care for men and women, sun care
Availability: professional skin care salons and clinics, day spas, physicians

Prescriptives, Inc. (Estée Lauder)
767 Fifth Ave.
New York, NY 10153
212-572-4400
Products: cosmetics, fragrance for women, skin care, sun care, toiletries, bathing supply, soap
Availability: department stores, specialty stores

Prestige Cosmetics
1441 W. Newport Center Dr.
Deerfield Beach, FL 33442
305-480-9202
800-722-7488
Products: cosmetics, nail care
Availability: drugstores, supermarkets, boutiques, specialty stores, beauty supply stores

Prestige Fragrances Ltd. (Revlon)
625 Madison Ave.
New York, NY 10022
212-572-5000
Products: fragrance for women
Availability: department stores

Principal Secret (Guthy Renker Corporation)
41-550 Ecclectic St., Suite 200
Palm Desert, CA 92260
800-545-5595
Products: skin care for men and women
Availability: J.C. Penney, home shopping networks, mail order
MO

Professional Pet Products, Inc.
1873 N.W. 97th Ave.
Miami, FL 33172
305-592-1992
800-432-5349
Products: companion animal care
Availability: companion animal supply stores, cooperatives, drugstores
V MO

Pro-Tec Pet Health
1717 Solano Way, Suite 17
Concord, CA 94520
510-676-9600
800-44-FLEAS
www.protec-pet-health.com
Products: companion animal care
Availability: companion animal supply stores, health food stores, groomers, feed stores, mail order
⭐ MO

P.S.I. Industries, Inc.
1619 Shenandoah Ave.
P.O. Box 4391
Roanoke, VA 24017
540-345-5013
Products: industrial odor/stain remover
Availability: distributors, mail order
MO

Pulse Products
2021 Ocean Ave., #105
Santa Monica, CA 90405
310-399-3447
310-392-0991
Products: massage oil
Availability: health food stores
V MO

Pure & Basic Products
20600 Belshaw Ave.
Carson, CA 90746
310-898-1630
800-432-3787
Products: hair care, toiletries, bathing supply, deodorant, soap, shaving supply, skin care, dandruff shampoo, air freshener, household, hypo-allergenic skin care for men and women
Availability: salons, beauty supply stores, cooperatives, mail order
V 🏠 MO

Pure Touch Therapeutic Body Care
P.O. Box 1281
Nevada City, CA 95959
800-442-7873
Products: fragrance for women, spa supply for massage professionals
Availability: health food stores, spas, distributors, mail order
V **MO**

Quan Yin Essentials
5333 Dry Creek Rd.
Healdsburg, CA 95448
707-431-0529
Products: fragrance for men and women, toiletries, skin care for men and women
Availability: health food stores, department stores, boutiques, specialty stores, gift stores, independent sales representatives, mail order
V **MO**

Queen Helene
100 Rose Ave.
Hempstead, NY 11550
516-538-4600
800-645-3752
www.queenhelene.com
Products: ethnic products, hair care, skin care, toiletries, bathing supply, deodorant, shaving supply, soap
Availability: department stores, discount department stores, drugstores, health food stores, supermarkets, cooperatives, mail order
MO

Rachel Perry, Inc.
9111 Mason Ave.
Chatsworth, CA 91311
818-888-5881
800-966-8888
www.rachelperry.net
Products: skin care, sun care, cosmetics
Availability: health food stores, beauty supply stores, Rachel Perry stores
★ **MO**

Rainbow Research Corporation
170 Wilbur Place
Bohemia, NY 11716
516-589-5563
800-722-9595
info@rainbowresearch.com
Products: baby care, hair care, hair color, hypo-allergenic skin care, toiletries, bathing supply, soap, massage oil
Availability: drugstores, health food stores, supermarkets, cooperatives, boutiques, specialty stores, mail order
MO

Rainforest Company
701 N. 15th St., Suite 500
St. Louis, MO 63103
314-621-1330
www.the-rainforest-co.com
Products: aromatherapy, hair care, toiletries, bathing supply, soap, rain forest-derived gifts
Availability: health food stores, boutiques, specialty stores
☒

Real Animal Friends
101 Albany Ave.
Freeport, NY 11520
516-223-7600
Products: companion animal care
Availability: companion animal supply stores, discount department stores, boutiques, specialty stores, mail order
V **MO**

Redken Laboratories, Inc.
575 Fifth Ave.
New York, NY 10017
212-818-1500
800-423-5369
Products: hair care, hair color, permanents, dandruff shampoo, hypo-allergenic skin care for men and women, toiletries, shaving supply, cosmetics, fragrance for women
Availability: salons
Note: Redkin does not test its products on animals. It may, however, test its ingredients on animals.

Redmond Products, Inc.
18930 W. 78th St.
Chanhassen, MN 55317
612-934-4868
800-328-0159
www.aussiehair.com
Products: hair care, Aussie, VitaMend
Availability: grocery stores, drugstores, beauty supply stores

---

Legend
V   Vegan (products contain no animal ingredients)
★   Company meets CSCA
☒   Company uses Caring Consumer product logo
MO   Mail order available

63

Reviva Labs, Inc.
705 Hopkins Rd.
Haddonfield, NJ 08033
609-428-3885
800-257-7774
Products: cosmetics, baby care, hair care, dandruff shampoo, sun care, hypoallergenic skin care for men and women, toiletries, shaving supply
Availability: health food stores, drugstores, discount department stores, supermarkets, cooperatives, boutiques, distributors, mail order
MO

Revlon, Inc.
625 Madison Ave.
New York, NY 10022
212-572-5000
800-473-8566
www.revlon.com
Products: cosmetics, ethnic products, toiletries, hair color, hair care, nail care, deodorant, Almay, Jean Naté, Flex, Outrageous, Ultima II
Availability: drugstores, department stores, supermarkets, beauty supply stores, discount department stores

Royal Labs Natural Cosmetics
Box 22434
Charleston, SC 29413
803-552-1504
800-760-7779
Products: aromatherapy, chemical-free cosmetics, hair care, hypo-allergenic skin care for men and women, sun care, toiletries, bathing supply, shaving supply
Availability: health food stores, supermarkets, boutiques, specialty stores, skin clinics, salons, spas
V MO

64

Rusk, Inc.
One Cummings Point Rd.
Stamford, CT 06904
203-316-4300
800-829-7875
www.rusk1.com
Products: hair care
Availability: salons

Sacred Blends
P.O. Box 634
Applegate, CA 95703
916-878-7464
888-722-7331
sacred1@softcom.net
Products: personal care, herbal salve, massage oil
Availability: health food stores, herb farms, mail order
★ MO

Safeway, Inc.
5918 Stoneridge Mall Rd.
Pleasanton, CA 94588
510-467-3000
Products: household, toiletries, baby care, toothbrushes
Availability: Safeway supermarkets

Sagami, Inc.
825 N. Cass Ave., Suite 101
Westmont, IL 60559
630-789-9999
Products: condoms (Excalibur, Sagami Type E, Vis-à-Vis, Peace & Sound regular, Peace & Sound ultra thin)
Availability: supermarkets, drugstores, specialty stores
V

Sanford Corporation
2711 Washington Blvd.
Bellwood, IL 60104
708-547-5525
800-323-0749
www.sanfordcorp.com
Products: office supply
Availability: drugstores, supermarkets, office supply stores, mail order
MO

San Francisco Soap Company
1129 Industrial Ave., Suite 200
Petaluma, CA 94952
707-769-5120
Products: skin care, toiletries, bathing supply, soap
Availability: department stores, health food stores, drugstores, supermarkets, cooperatives, mail order
MO

Santa Fe Botanical Fragrances, Inc.
P.O. Box 282
Santa Fe, NM 87501
505-473-1717
perfume@NewMexico.com
Products: botanical cologne, fragrance for men and women, aromatherapy
Availability: natural food stores, mail order
V MO

Legend

V — Vegan (products contain no animal ingredients)
★ — Company meets CSCA
🐰 — Company uses Caring Consumer product logo
MO — Mail order available

▼SANFORD®
THE MARK OF QUALITY

Environmentally Friendly. • No Animal Testing.

©1998 Sanford, Bellwood, Illinois 60104   www.sanfordcorp.com   A newell Company.

Santa Fe Soap Company
369 Montezuma, #167
Santa Fe, NM 87501
505-986-6064
888-SOAPBAR
Products: hair care, toiletries, soap
Availability: department stores, health food stores, supermarkets, cooperatives, boutiques, specialty stores, independent sales representatives, bath shops, mail order
V MO

Sappo Hill Soapworks
654 Tolman Creek Rd.
Ashland, OR 97520
541-482-4485
Products: soap
Availability: health food stores
V

Schiff Products, Inc.
1960 S. 4250 W.
Salt Lake City, UT 84104
801-972-0300
800-444-5200
Products: vitamin and mineral supplements
Availability: health food stores, mail order
MO

Scruples, Inc.
8231 214th St. W.
Lakeville, MN 55044
612-469-4646
Products: hair care, hair color, permanents
Availability: salons

Sea-renity
c/o Israel Business Centers
Tel-Aviv Hilton, Independence Park
Tel-Aviv, Israel 63405
972-3-520-22
Products: aromatherapy, skin and spa care for men and women, bath salts, Dead Sea black mud body wraps, holistic scrubs, shower gel, soap
Availability: health food stores, cooperatives, boutiques, specialty stores, distributors, mail order
MO

Sebastian International, Inc.
6109 DeSoto Ave.
Woodland Hills, CA 91367
818-999-5112
800-829-7322
Products: hair care, hair color, skin care for women
Availability: salons, Sebastian collective salon members

SerVaas Laboratories
P.O. Box 7008
1200 Waterway Blvd.
Indianapolis, IN 46207
317-636-7760
800-433-5818
Products: household
Availability: supermarkets, discount department stores, drugstores
V

Seventh Generation
One Mill St.
Burlington, VT 05401-1530
802-658-3773
800-456-1177
Products: baby care, nonchlorine bleach, feminine hygiene, household, laundry detergent, dish detergent, 100% recycled paper products
Availability: health food stores, supermarkets, cooperatives, mail order
V MO

Shadow Lake, Inc.
P.O. Box 2597
Danbury, CT 06813-2597
203-778-0881
800-343-6588
Products: aromatherapy, baby care, household, air freshener, carpet cleaning supply, oven cleaner, toiletries, bathing supply, soap
Availability: discount department stores, health food stores, supermarkets, cooperatives, boutiques, specialty stores, mail order
V MO

Shahin Soap Company
427 Van Dyke Ave.
Haledon, NJ 07508
201-790-4296
Products: soap
Availability: mail order
V MO

Shaklee Corporation
444 Market St.
San Francisco, CA 94111
415-954-3000
800-SHAKLEE
Products: baby care, cosmetics, dental hygiene, fragrance, hair care, household, laundry detergent, hypo-allergenic skin care, sun care, toiletries, bathing supply, shaving supply, deodorant, soap, garden supply
Availability: independent sales representatives

Shene Cosmetics
22761 Pacific Coast Hwy.
Suite 264
P.O. Box 2206
Malibu, CA 90265
800-315-1967
Products: sun protection cosmetics, nail care, toiletries
Availability: discount department stores, mail order
MO

```
Legend
V   Vegan (products
    contain no animal
    ingredients)
★   Company meets
    CSCA
    Company uses
    Caring Consumer
    product logo
MO  Mail order
    available
```

Shikai (Trans-India Products)
P.O. Box 2866
Santa Rosa, CA 95405
707-544-0298
800-448-0298
Products: hair care, hair styling, hand and body lotion, shower and bath gel for men and women, color-enhancing shampoo, skin care
Availability: drugstores, health food stores, supermarkets, cooperatives, boutiques, specialty stores
MO

Shirley Price Aromatherapy
P.O. Box 65
Pineville, PA 18946
215-598-3802
Products: hypo-allergenic skin care for men and women, pure essential oil of therapeutic quality
Availability: massage therapists, salons, spas, health food stores, mail order
MO

Shivani Ayurvedic Cosmetics (Devi, Inc.)
P.O. Box 377
Lancaster, MA 01523
508-368-0066
800-237-8221
skmas@aol.com
Products: aromatherapy, cosmetics, fragrance, hair care, skin care, toiletries, soap
Availability: health food stores, cooperatives, mail order
MO

Simplers Botanical Company
P.O. Box 39
6450 First St.
Forestville, CA 95436
707-887-7570
800-6JASMIN
Products: Sierra Sage Salves, aromatherapy, companion animal care, herbal extracts, personal care
Availability: mail order, health food stores
V 🖐 MO

Simple Wisdom, Inc.
775 S. Graham
Memphis, TN 38111
901-458-4686
Products: toiletries, hair care, skin care for men and women, massage oil, perfume oil, essential oil, fragrance for women, household, liquid soap, spot remover
Availability: health food stores, cooperatives, boutiques, specialty stores, mail order
MO

Sinclair & Valentine
480 Airport Blvd.
Watsonville, CA 95076-2056
408-722-9526
Products: aromatherapy, baby care, household, air freshener, skin care for women, toiletries, bathing supply, soap
Availability: discount department stores, drugstores, health food stores, supermarkets

Sirena (Tropical Soap Company)
P.O. Box 112220
Carrollton, TX 75011
214-357-1464
800-527-2368
Products: Sirena liquid and bar soaps
Availability: health food stores, mail order
V MO

Smith & Vandiver
480 Airport Blvd.
Watsonville, CA 95076-2056
408-722-9526
800-722-1434
Products: aromatherapy, baby care, cosmetics, fragrance for women, hair care, skin care, sun care, toiletries, bathing supply, soap, shaving supply, home fragrance
Availability: department stores, drugstores, health food stores, boutiques, specialty stores

SoapBerry Shop Company
50 Galaxy Blvd., Unit 12
Rexdale, ON M9W 4Y5
Canada
416-213-0802
Products: hair care, sun care, cosmetics, toothbrushes, baby care, hypoallergenic skin care for men and women, toiletries, shaving supply, dental hygiene, fragrance for men and women, nail care
Availability: SoapBerry Shop stores, mail order
MO

Soap Opera
319 State St.
Madison, WI 53703
608-251-4051
800-251-7627
Thesoapop@aol.com
Products: aromatherapy, toothbrushes, fragrance, hair care, hair color, personal care, deodorant
Availability: The Soap Opera store, mail order
★ MO

Sojourner Farms Natural Pet Products
11355 Excelsior Blvd.
Hopkins, MN 55343
612-935-2312
888-867-6567
holistic@visi.com
Products: natural companion animal care, food, and supply
Availability: health food stores, cooperatives, companion animal supply stores, mail order
MO

Solgar Vitamin Company
500 Willow Tree Rd.
Leonia, NJ 07605
201-944-2311
www.solgar.com
Products: vitamins
Availability: health food stores, cooperatives

Sombra Cosmetics, Inc.
5600-G McLeod N.E.
Albuquerque, NM 87109
505-888-0288
800-225-3963
Products: cosmetics, skin care, theatrical makeup
Availability: health food stores, mail order
MO

THE SOAP OPERA

BAUER & BECKWITH®

319 STATE STREET • MADISON WI 53703
THE LAST WORD IN QUALITY • SELECTION • SERVICE

Dear Friends,

To each of you we promise to offer only 100% biodegradable, cruelty free (no animal testing) products based on earth-friendly, safe, effective ingredients, continuing our business philosophy unchanged for over a quarter of a century! (Everything is 100% guaranteed, of course.)

Sincerely, and with thanks,

Chuck Bauer

Chuck Beckwith

Co-Founders (March 3, 1972) & Co-Owners

Call 800-251-7627 for a
FREE CATALOG

PHONE (608) 251-4051 • FAX (608) 251-1703
www.thesoapopera.com

SoRik International
278 Taileyand Ave.
Jacksonville, FL 32202
904-353-4200
800-824-8255
Products: hair care, sun care, toiletries
Availability: salons
MO

Soya System, Inc.
10441 Midwest Industrial
St. Louis, MO 63132
314-428-0004
www.soya.com
Products: hair care, permanents
Availability: salons, beauty supply stores

Spa Natural Beauty Products
1201 16th St., #212
Denver, CO 80202
800-598-3878
Products: cosmetics, hypo-allergenic skin care for men and women, sun care, toiletries, hair care, fragrance for women
Availability: Spa Natural Beauty Products stores, mail order
MO

Spanish Bath
P.O. Box 750428
Petaluma, CA 94975-0428
707-769-5120
Products: toiletries, bath gel, body lotion, mineral salt
Availability: discount department stores, cooperatives, health food stores, drugstores, boutiques, specialty stores, mail order
V MO

Staedtler, Ltd.
Cowbridge Rd.
Pontyclym, Mid Glamorgan
Wales
0448 237421
Products: writing instruments, office supply
Availability: office supply stores in the U.K.

Stanhome, Inc.
50 Payson Ave.
Easthampton, MA 01027-2262
413-527-4001
Products: household
Availability: hardware stores, distributors

Steps in Health, Ltd.
P.O. Box 1409
Lake Grove, NY 11755
516-471-2432
800-471-8343
Products: companion animal care, dental hygiene, hair care, household, air freshener, skin care for women, toiletries, deodorant, soap, vitamins
Availability: mail order
MO

Stevens Research Salon Products
19417 63rd Ave. N.E.
Arlington, WA 98223
360-435-4513
800-262-3344
Products: hair care, permanents
Availability: salons, beauty schools
V

Studio Magic Cosmetics
20135 Cypress Creek Dr.
Alva, FL 33920-3305
941-728-3344
800-452-7706
studiomagic@worldnet.att.net
Products: aromatherapy, cosmetics, hypo-allergenic skin care, sun care, theatrical makeup, vitamins, herbs
Availability: Studio Magic stores, boutiques, specialty stores, independent sales representatives, physicians, salons, mail order
🖾 MO

Sukesha
P.O. Box 5126
Manchester, NH 03108
603-669-4228
800-221-3496
Products: hair care, hair color, permanents
Availability: salons

Sumeru
P.O. Box 1008
Silver Lake, WI 53170
800-478-6378
www.international.com
Products: aromatherapy, baby care, personal care
Availability: health food stores, mail order
V MO

Legend
V   Vegan (products contain no animal ingredients)
★   Company meets CSCA
🖾   Company uses Caring Consumer product logo
MO Mail order available

69

SunFeather Natural Soap Company
1551 Highway 72
Potsdam, NY 13676
315-265-3648
800-771-7627
www.electroniccottage.com/sunfeathersoaps/
Products: aromatherapy, baby care, companion animal care, shampoo bars, insect repellant, soap-making supply, personal care, modeling soap for children
Availability: department stores, drugstores, health food stores, cooperatives, boutiques, specialty stores, independent sales representatives
V 🕭 MO

Sunrider International
1625 Abalone Ave.
Torrance, CA 90501
310-781-3808
Products: cosmetics, dental hygiene, fragrance, hair care, household, nail care, skin care, sun care, toiletries, bathing supply, soap, shaving supply, vitamins
Availability: independent sales representatives

Sunrise Lane
780 Greenwich St., Dept. PT
New York, NY 10014
212-242-7014
fyman@dpw.com
Products: baby care, dental hygiene, hair care, hair color, permanents, household, bleach, carpet cleaning supply, laundry detergent, hypo-allergenic skin care, bathing supply, shaving supply, deodorant, soap
Availability: mail order
MO

Sunshine Natural Products
Rte. 5P
Renick, WV 24966
304-497-3163
Products: companion animal care, hair care, dandruff shampoo
Availability: health food stores, cooperatives
V MO

Sunshine Products Group
2545-A Prairie Rd.
Eugene, OR 97402
503-461-2160
800-285-6457
Products: essential oil, herbal oil, body lotion, massage oil, aromatherapy
Availability: health food stores, drugstores, mail order
V MO

Supreme Beauty Products Company
820 S. Michigan
Chicago, IL 60605
312-322-0670
800-272-6602
Products: hair care
Availability: drugstores, mail order
MO

Surrey, Inc.
13110 Trails End Rd.
Leander, TX 78641
512-267-7172
Products: toiletries, shaving supply
Availability: health food stores, drugstores, department stores, discount department stores, supermarkets, distributors
🕭

Tammy Taylor Nails
18007E Skypark Cir.
Irvine, CA 92714
714-756-6606
800-748-6665
Products: cosmetics, skin care, hypo-allergenic skin care, nail care, sun care, toiletries
Availability: Tammy Taylor stores, mail order, distributors
MO

TauT by Leonard Engelman
9428 Eton, #M
Chatsworth, CA 91311
818-773-3975
800-438-8288
Products: cosmetics, hypo-allergenic skin care for men and women, sun care, theatrical makeup, toiletries, bathing supply
Availability: health food stores, beauty supply stores, salons, mail order
MO

Terra Nova
1200 Fifth St.
Berkeley, CA 94710
510-528-0666
Products: fragrance, skin care, toiletries, shaving supply, soap, massage oil and lotion
Availability: department stores, drugstores, health food stores, boutiques, specialty stores

Terressentials
2650 Old National Pike
Middletown, MD 21769-8817
301-371-7333
Products: cosmetics, fragrance for men and women, hair care, hair color, household, air freshener, insect repellant, skin care, bathing supply, deodorant, shaving supply, soap, vitamins, herbs
Availability: health food stores, Terressentials stores, boutiques, specialty stores, mail order
V MO

Thursday Plantation Party Ltd.
330 E. Carrillo
Santa Barbara, CA 93101
805-963-2297
800-645-9500
Products: toiletries, dental hygiene, hair care, dandruff shampoo, hypo-allergenic skin care for men and women, sun care
Availability: health food stores, drugstores, supermarkets

Tish & Snooky's Manic Panic
64-66 White St., 3rd Fl.
New York, NY 10013
212-941-0656
800-95-MANIC
Products: cosmetics, hair bleach, hair color, nail care
Availability: health food stores, department stores, mail order, drugstores
MO

Tisserand Aromatherapy, USA
P.O. Box 750428
Petaluma, CA 94975-0428
707-769-5120
Products: pure essential oil, hair care, massage oil and lotion, skin care for men and women, toiletries, aromatherapy
Availability: department stores, health food stores, boutiques, specialty stores, salons, spas, mail order
V MO

Tom's of Maine
P.O. Box 710
302 Lafayette Ctr.
Kennebunk, ME 04043
207-985-2944
800-367-8667
www.toms-of-maine.com
Products: baby care, dental hygiene, hair care, toiletries, deodorant, shaving supply, soap
Availability: drugstores, health food stores, supermarkets, cooperatives, Tom's of Maine stores, boutiques, specialty stores, mail order
★ MO

> **Legend**
> **V** Vegan (products contain no animal ingredients)
> **★** Company meets CSCA
> 🖐 Company uses Caring Consumer product logo
> **MO** Mail order available

Tova Corporation
192 N. Canon Dr.
Beverly Hills, CA 90210
310-246-0218
Products: skin care, hair care, fragrance
Availability: QVC, department stores, boutiques

Trader Joe's Company
P.O. Box 3270
538 Mission St.
South Pasadena, CA 91030
818-441-1777
Products: hair care, household, toiletries
Availability: Trader Joe's Company stores

Travel Mates America
23750 St. Clair Ave.
Cleveland, OH 44117
216-738-2222
Products: hair care, toiletries
Availability: private label for hotel-industry products only

Tressa, Inc.
P.O. Box 75320
Cincinnati, OH 45275
606-525-1300
800-879-8737
Products: hair care
Availability: professional beauty salons

TRI Hair Care Products
1850 Redondo Ave.
Long Beach, CA 90804
562-494-6300
800-458-8874
Products: hair care
Availability: salons, mail order
MO

71

Trophy Animal Health Care
2796 Helen St.
Pensacola, FL 32504
904-476-7087
800-336-7087
Products: companion animal care
Availability: select distributors, select companion animal supply stores, mail order
MO

Tropix Suncare Products
217 S. Seventh St., Suite 104
Brainerd, MN 56401
800-421-7314
Products: sun care
Availability: tanning salons
V

Truly Moist (Desert Naturels, Inc.)
74-940 Hwy. 111, Suite 437
Indian Wells, CA 92201
619-346-1604
800-243-4435
Products: hypo-allergenic skin care for men and women
Availability: health food stores, drugstores

Tyra Skin Care for Men and Women, Inc.
9424 Eaton Ave., Suite J
Chatsworth, CA 91311
818-407-1274
Products: hypo-allergenic skin care for men and women, sun care
Availability: department stores, boutiques, specialty stores, mail order
MO

The Ultimate Life
P.O. Box 4308
Santa Barbara, CA 93140
805-962-2221
800-843-6325
www.ultimatelife.com
Products: instant meals offering optimum nutrition, vitamins, herbs
Availability: health food stores, mail order, health care practitioners, health clubs
V 🢐 MO

Ultima II (Revlon)
625 Madison Ave.
New York, NY 10022
212-572-5000
Products: cosmetics
Availability: department stores

Ultra Glow Cosmetics (Nickull-Dowdall)
P.O. Box 1469, Station A
Vancouver, BC V6C 2P7
Canada
604-939-3329
Products: cosmetics, sun care, theatrical makeup
Availability: drugstores, department stores, boutiques, specialty stores, mail order
V MO

Upper Canada Soap & Candle Makers
1510 Caterpillar Rd.
Mississauga, ON L4X 2W9
Canada
905-897-1710
Products: toiletries, soap
Availability: gift stores

Urban Decay
345 California St., Suite 3300
San Francisco, CA 94104
650-988-9969
800-784-URBAN
www.urbandecay.com
Products: cosmetics, hair color, nail care, theatrical makeup
Availability: discount department stores, boutiques, specialty stores
★ MO

USA King's Crossing, Inc.
P.O. Box 832074
Richardson, TX 75083
972-680-9663
www.shaveking.com
Products: all-natural shaving oil, razors, razor blades, skin care for men and women
Availability: health food stores, mail order, specialty stores, drugstores
V 🢐 MO

U.S. Sales Service (Crystal Orchid)
374 W. Citation
Tempe, AZ 85284
602-839-3761
800-487-2633
Products: deodorant stones, soap
Availability: health food stores, cooperatives, independent sales representatives, mail order
V 🢐 MO

Vapor Products
P.O. Box 568395
Orlando, FL 32856-8395
407-851-6230
800-621-2943
Products: mold and mildew prevention, household
Availability: discount department stores, supermarkets, Home Depot
MO

Vermont Soapworks
76 Exchange St.
Middlebury, VT 05753
802-388-4302
www.vtsoap.com
Products: aromatherapy, baby care, household, soap
Availability: health food stores, cooperatives, supermarkets, department stores, specialty stores, drugstores, mail order
MO

Veterinarian's Best, Inc.
P.O. Box 4459
Santa Barbara, CA 93103
805-963-5609
800-866-PETS
vetsbest@aol.com
Products: companion animal care
Availability: health food stores, supermarkets, companion animal supply stores, groomers, companion animal catalogs
V MO

Victoria's Secret
4 Limited Pkwy.
Reynoldsburg, OH 43068
614-577-7111
www.limited.com
Products: toiletries, fragrance and skin care for women, sun care
Availability: Victoria's Secret stores
MO

Virginia Soap, Ltd.
Group 60, Box 20, R.R. 1
Anola, MB R0E 0A0
Canada
204-866-3788
Products: toiletries, aromatherapy
Availability: health food stores, drugstores, gift stores, mail order
MO

Legend

V — Vegan (products contain no animal ingredients)
★ — Company meets CSCA
☕ — Company uses Caring Consumer product logo
MO — Mail order available

Personal care performers ... for you and your customers

".. not only a great idea, but a consistent seller too!"
Gary Schuyler
Retail Manager
Moments, Ltd.

Crystal Orchid®
Loofa Soap

"Thank you so much for such a useful product."
Elnora T. Brown
Humble, TX

Crystal Orchid®
Deodorant Stone
1-800 487-2633

US Sales Service

Gentle On You
Gentle On The Earth™

- Bar Soaps
- Liquid Soaps
- Non Toxic Cleaners
- Cruelty Free
- All Natural
- Biodegradable
- Free Catalog Available

Vermont Soapworks
76 Exchange Street Middlebury, VT 05753
Phone: (802) 388-4302   Fax: (802) 388-7471
Web Site: www.vtsoap.com

Von Myering by Krystina
208 Seville Ave.
Pittsburgh, PA 15214
412-766-3186
Products: skin care, hair care, permanents, hair color
Availability: health food stores, salons, mail order
V MO

V'tae Parfum & Body Care
571 Searls Ave.
Nevada City, CA 95959
916-265-4255
800-643-3011
www.vtae.com
Products: aromatherapy, fragrance, household, air freshener, insect repellant, toiletries, bathing supply, soap, candles, massage oil, lotion
Availability: department stores, drugstores, health food stores, cooperatives, V'tae Parfum & Body Care stores, boutiques, specialty stores
MO

Wachters' Organic Sea Products
360 Shaw Rd.
S. San Francisco, CA 94080
650-588-9567
800-682-7100
wachter.osp@aol.com
Products: aromatherapy, companion animal care, hair care, laundry detergent, skin care for men and women, toiletries, bathing supply, vitamins, herbs
Availability: independent sales representatives, mail order, natural food stores
MO

Legend
- **V** Vegan (products contain no animal ingredients)
- ★ Company meets CSCA
- 🐇 Company uses Caring Consumer product logo
- **MO** Mail order available

Wala-Heilmittel
P.O. Box 407
Wyoming, RI 02898
401-539-7037
800-499-7037
Products: skin care, toiletries
Availability: health food stores

Warm Earth Cosmetics
1155 Stanley Ave.
Chico, CA 95928-6944
530-895-0455
warmearth@aol.com
Products: cosmetics, fragrance for men, toiletries, deodorant
Availability: health food stores, drugstores, supermarkets, boutiques, specialty stores, mail order
MO

Weleda, Inc.
P.O. Box 249
Congers, NY 10920
914-268-8572
800-289-1969
www.weleda.com
Products: aromatherapy, baby care, dental hygiene, hair care, skin care, toiletries, bathing supply, deodorant, soap
Availability: drugstores, health food stores, supermarkets, cooperatives, Weleda stores, boutiques, specialty stores, mail order
MO

Wella Corporation
12 Mercedes Dr.
Montvale, NJ 07645
201-930-1020
800-526-4657
Products: hair care, hair color, permanents
Availability: salons

Wellington Laboratories, Inc.
1147 Stoneshead Ct., Suite B
Westlake Village, CA 91361
805-495-4824
800-835-8118
Products: baby care, hypoallergenic skin care, toiletries, shaving supply
Availability: distributors, drugstores, supermarkets, boutiques, specialty stores, discount department stores, department stores, cooperatives
MO

Whip-It Products, Inc.
P.O. Box 30128
Pensacola, FL 32503
904-436-2125
800-582-0398
Products: all-purpose cleaning supply for home and industrial use, oven cleaning supply, carpet cleaning supply, laundry detergent
Availability: independent sales representatives, mail order
V MO

Wind River Herbs
P.O. Box 3876
Jackson, WY 83001
307-733-6731
Products: herbal medicine
Availability: The Herb Store, health food stores, clinics
MO

Wisdom Toothbrush Company
151 S. Pfingsten Rd.
Deerfield, IL 60015
847-272-2040
800-628-4798
70702.1765@compuserve.com
Products: dental hygiene, toothbrushes, dental floss
Availability: drugstores, mail order, dentists
MO

WiseWays Herbals
Singing Brook Farm
99 Harvey Rd.
Worthington, MA 01098
413-238-4268
888-540-1600
Products: aromatherapy, baby care, companion animal care, hair care, air freshener, furniture oil, insect repellant, bathing supply, skin care, soap
Availability: drugstores, health food stores, supermarkets, cooperatives, boutiques, specialty stores, independent sales representatives, mail order
MO

Womankind
P.O. Box 1775
Sebastopol, CA 95473
707-522-8662
wkind@wco.com
Products: cloth menstrual pads, feminine hygiene
Availability: health food stores, supermarkets, boutiques, independent sales representatives, specialty stores, cooperatives, mail order
MO

Zia Cosmetics Natural Skincare

To Make Your Skin Look Good, It Has To Be Good For Your Skin.

CRUELTY-FREE. UNCONDITIONALLY GUARANTEED.
AT NATURAL FOOD STORES OR CALL 1.800.334.7546

Wysong Corporation
1880 N. Eastman Rd.
Midland, MI 48642-7779
517-631-0009
800-748-0188
wysong@tm.net
Products: hair care, sun care, vitamins, toiletries, shaving supply
Availability: health food stores
MO

Zia Cosmetics
1337 Evans Ave.
San Francisco, CA 94124
415-642-8339
800-334-7546
Products: aromatherapy, cosmetics, skin care for men and women, sun care
Availability: drugstores, health food stores, cooperatives, boutiques, specialty stores
MO

Legend

V Vegan (products contain no animal ingredients)

★ Company meets CSCA

▩ Company uses Caring Consumer product logo

MO Mail order available

Catalogs/Stores Offering Cruelty-Free Products

The following catalog companies and stores offer products not tested on animals.

The Caring Catalog
7678 Sagewood Dr.
Huntington Beach, CA 92648
714-842-0454
ccwest@gte.net

Green Earth Office Supply
P.O. Box 719
Redwood Estates, CA 95044
800-327-8449
www.webcom.com/geos/

Heritage Store, Inc.
P.O. Box 444
Virginia Beach, VA 23458
757-428-0100
800-862-2923

NOHARM (formerly WARM Store)
119 Turkey Hill Rd.
Northampton, MA 01062
413-587-0789
www.orbyss.com/noharm.htm

Pangea Vegan Products
7829 Woodmont Ave.
Bethesda, MD 20814
301-652-3181
pangeaveg@aol.com

PETA
501 Front St.
Norfolk, VA 23510
757-622-7382
www.peta-online.org

Salon Advantage
614 E. Hwy. 50, #320
Clermont, FL 34711
352-243-0636
Salonadvtg@aol.com

Veg Essentials
7722 W. Menomonee River Pkwy.
Wauwatosa, WI 53213
414-607-1953
877-881-6477

Quick Reference Guide

AIR FRESHENER

Amway Corporation	15
Ananda Collection	15
Aroma Vera	16
Astonish Industries	16
Auroma International	17
Ayurherbal Corporation	18
Basically Natural	18
Bath and Body Works	19
Bella's Secret Garden	20
Body Time	22
Botanicus Retail	22
Common Scents	26
Compassion Matters	27
Crabtree & Evelyn	28
CYA Products	28
Dr. Singha's	30
Earth Friendly	30
Earthly Matters	32
Ecco Bella Botanicals	32
Essential Products of America	34
Every Body	35
Harvey Universal	39
Herbal Products	40
Liberty Natural	49
Mère Cie	51
Mother's Little Miracle	52
Natura	53
Natural World	54
No Common Scents	57
Orange-Mate	58
Oxyfresh Worldwide	59
Pathmark Stores	59
PlantEssence	60
Potions & Lotions	62
Pure & Basic Products	62
Shadow Lake	66
Sinclair & Valentine	67
Steps in Health	69
Terressentials	71
V'tae Parfum	74
WiseWays Herbals	75

AROMATHERAPY

ABBA Products	11
Abra Therapeutics	11
Ahimsa	11
Alexandra Avery	11
American Safety Razor	13
Apothecary Shoppe	15
Aromaland	16
Aroma Vera	16
Atmosa Brand Aromatherapy	17
Aura Cacia	17
Australasian College	18
Autumn-Harp	18
Bare Escentuals	18
Basically Natural	18
Bath and Body Works	19
Bath Island	19
Beauty Without Cruelty Cosmetics	20
Belle Star	20
Better Botanicals	20
Biotone	21
Body Encounters	21
Body Shop	21
Body Time	22
Börland of Germany	22
Bronzo Sensualé	22
Caswell-Massey	24
Celestial Body	25
Columbia Cosmetics	26
Common Scents	26
Compassion Matters	27
Countryside Fragrances	28
Derma-E	29
Dermalogica	29
Desert Essence	30
Dr. Singha's	30
Earth Science	32
Ecco Bella Botanicals	32
Elizabeth Van Buren	34
Enfasi Hair Care	34
Essential Aromatics	34
Essential Oil Company	34

Essential Products of America	34
EuroZen	35
Every Body	35
Faces by Gustavo	35
Faith Products	35
For Pet's Sake	36
Frontier Natural Products	37
Herb Garden	40
Home Health Products	40
Jeanne Rose Aromatherapy	42
Katonah Scentral	45
La Crista	47
Lady of the Lake	47
Lander Company	47
Lissée Cosmetics	50
Lotus Light	50
Mère Cie	51
Mia Rose Products	52
Montagne Jeunesse	52
Natura	53
Natural Bodycare	54
Natural Science	54
Natural World	54
Nirvana	57
Potions & Lotions	62
Rainforest Company	63
Royal Labs	64
Santa Fe Botanical	64
Sea-renity	65
Shadow Lake	66
Shivani Ayurvedic Cosmetics	66
Simplers Botanical	67
Sinclair & Valentine	67
Smith & Vandiver	67
Soap Opera	67
Sumeru	69
SunFeather Natural Soap	70
Sunshine Products Group	70
Tisserand Aromatherapy	71
Vermont Soapworks	73
Virginia Soap	73
V'tae Parfum	74
Wachters'	74

Weleda	75
WiseWays Herbals	75
Zia Cosmetics	76

BABY CARE

Ahimsa	11
Alexandra Avery	11
Amway	15
Arizona Natural Resources	15
Aubrey Organics	17
Aura Cacia	17
Autumn-Harp	18
Bath and Body Works	19
Bath Island	19
Baudelaire	19
Bella's Secret Garden	20
Better Botanicals	20
Body Shop	21
Body Time	22
Caeran	24
Caswell-Massey	24
Common Scents	26
Compassion Matters	27
Country Comfort	27
Crabtree & Evelyn	28
Dermatologic Cosmetic Laboratories	30
Dr. Bronner's	30
Earth Solutions	32
Essential Oil Company	34
Every Body	35
Faces by Gustavo	35
For Pet's Sake	36
Healthy Times	40
Jurlique	45
Katonah Scentral	45
Kiehl's Since 1851	46
Kiss My Face	46
KSA Jojoba	46
La Crista	47
LaNatura	47
Lander Company	47
Liberty Natural	49
Logona USA	50
Lotus Light	50
Magick Botanicals	51
Mother's Little Miracle	52
Mountain Ocean	52

Naturade Cosmetics	53
Natural Science	54
North Country Soap	57
Potions & Lotions	62
Rainbow Research	63
Reviva Labs	64
Safeway	64
Seventh Generation	66
Shadow Lake	66
Shaklee	66
Sinclair & Valentine	67
Smith & Vandiver	67
SoapBerry Shop Company	67
Sumeru	69
Sunfeather Natural Soap	70
Sunrise Lane	70
Tom's of Maine	71
Vermont Soapworks	73
Weleda	75
Wellington	75
WiseWays Herbals	75

BAKING SODA

Frontier Natural Products	37
Pathmark Stores	59

BLEACH

Amway	15
Basically Natural	18
Bio Pac	21
Country Save	27
Ecover	32
Home Service Products	41
Huish Detergents	41
James Austin Company	42
Kleen Brite	46
Seventh Generation	66
Sunrise Lane	70

CAR CARE

Amway	15
Caeran	24
CHIP Distribution	25
For Pet's Sake	36

IQ Products Company	42
Natural World	54
Nature Clean	54
Shadow Lake	66

CARPET CLEANING

Advanage	11
American Formulating	13
Amway	15
Astonish Industries	16
Bio Pac	21
Caeran	24
CHIP Distribution	25
Crown Royale	28
Earthly Matters	32
Forever Living	36
Greenway Products	39
Harvey Universal	39
James Austin Company	42
Lightning Products	49
Marché Image	51
Natural World	54
Nature Clean	54
Pet Connection	60
Pets 'n People (Nature's Miracle)	60
Shadow Lake	66
Sunrise Lane	70
Whip-It Products	75

COMPANION ANIMAL CARE

Aubrey Organics	17
Ayurveda Holistic Center	18
Basically Natural	18
Brookside Soap Company	22
Bug Off	22
Caeran	24
Carina Supply	24
Crown Royale	28
Dallas Manufacturing	28
Dr. A. C. Daniels	30
Dr. Bronner's	30
Dr. Goodpet	30
Earth Solutions	32
Eco Design Company	32

79

Epilady International	34	**CONDOMS/LUBRICANTS**		Clientele	26
Essential Aromatics	34			Clinique	26
Fleabusters	36	BioFilm	20	Color Me Beautiful	26
Forever Living	36	Bronzo Sensualé	22	Color My Image	26
Green Ban	39	InterNatural	42	Columbia Cosmetics	26
Greentree Laboratories	39	Jason Natural Cosmetics	42	Compassionate	
Greenway Products	39	Lotus Light	50	Consumer	27
Halo Purely for Pets	39	Sagami	64	Compassionate	
Herb Garden	40			Cosmetics	27
Hewitt Soap Company	40			Compassion Matters	27
Home Health Products	40	**CONTACT LENS**		Concept Now Cosmetics	27
Jeanne Rose Aromatherapy	42	**SOLUTION**		Cosmair	27
K.B. Products	46			Cosmyl	27
Kenic Pet Products	46	Lobob Laboratories	50	Decleor USA	28
KSA Jojoba	46			Diamond Brands	30
Lightning Products	49			Dr. Hauschka	30
Lotus Light	50	**COSMETICS**		E. Burnham Cosmetics	32
Mallory Pet Supplies	51			Ecco Bella Botanicals	32
Mr. Christal's	53	Adrien Arpel	11	Elizabeth Grady	34
Nala Barry Labs	53	Alexandra de Markoff	12	Enfasi Hair Care	34
Naturade Cosmetics	53	Almay	12	Estée Lauder	34
Natural Chemistry	54	Aloette	12	Eva Jon Cosmetics	35
Naturally Yours, Alex	54	Alvin Last	13	Every Body	35
Natural Products	54	Amway	15	Faces by Gustavo	35
Natural Research People	54	Arbonne International	15	Fernand Aubry	36
Nature's Best	55	Arizona Natural	15	Finelle Cosmetics	36
Nature's Country Pet	55	Aubrey Organics	17	For Pet's Sake	36
Nature's Plus	55	Autumn-Harp	18	Garden Botanika	37
No Common Scents	57	Aveda	18	Georgette Klinger	37
North Country Soap	57	Avon	18	Hard Candy	39
N/R Laboratories	57	Bare Escentuals	18	Helen Lee Skin Care	40
Nutri-Cell	58	Basically Natural	18	H2O Plus	41
Oxyfresh Worldwide	59	Bath and Body Works	19	Ida Grae	41
Pet Connection	60	BeautiControl	19	Il-Makiage	41
PetGuard	60	Beauty Without Cruelty	20	Ilona	41
Pets 'n People	60	Beverly Hills Cosmetic		i natural cosmetics	
Professional Pet Products	62	Group	20	(Cosmetic Source)	41
Pro-Tec Pet Health	62	Bio-Tec Cosmetics	21	InterNatural	42
Real Animal Friends	63	Bobbi Brown	21	Jennifer Tara	45
Simplers Botanical	67	Bodyography	21	Joe Blasco Cosmetics	45
Sojourner Farms	67	Body Shop	21	Jurlique	45
Steps in Health	69	Bonne Bell	22	Kiehl's Since 1851	46
SunFeather Natural Soap	70	Börlind of Germany	22	Kiss My Face	46
Sunshine Natural Products	70	Bronson Pharmaceuticals	22	KSA Jojoba	46
Trophy Animal Health		Candy Kisses	24	La Costa Products	46
Care	72	Chanel	25	LaNatura	47
Veterinarian's Best	73	Christian Dior	25	Lancôme	47
Wachters'	74	Christine Valmy	25	La Prairie	49
WiseWays Herbals	75	CiCi Cosmetics	25	Lissée Cosmetics	50
		Cinema Secrets	25	L'Oréal	50
		Clarins of Paris	25	Lotus Light	50
				M.A.C.	50

Magic of Aloe	51		**DANDRUFF SHAMPOO**			**DENTAL HYGIENE**	
Marilyn Miglin Institute	51						
Maybelline	51		Ahimsa	11		Alvin Last	13
Mehron	51		Alvin Last	13		Amway	15
Merle Norman	52		Amway	15		Auroma International	17
Mira Linder Spa	52		Avon	18		Auromère Ayurvedic	
Narwhale of High Tor	53		Bath Island	19		Imports	18
Naturade Cosmetics	53		Beauty Naturally	20		Ayurherbal Corporation	18
Natural Science	54		Brocato International	22		Bath Island	19
Nature's Acres	54		Caeran	24		Baudelaire	19
Nature's Plus	55		Carina Supply	24		Beehive Botanicals	20
Neways	57		Citré Shine	25		Body Shop	21
Nutri-Metics	58		Compassion Matters	27		Caswell-Massey	24
Ohio Hempery	58		Creighton's Naturally	28		Comfort Manufacturing	26
Oriflame Corporation	58		Decleor USA	28		Common Scents	26
Origins Natural			Derma-E	29		Compassion Matters	27
Resources	58		Dermatologic Cosmetic			Desert Essence	30
Orjene Natural			Laboratories	30		Eco-Dent	32
Cosmetics	58		Ecco Bella Botanicals	32		Eco Design Company	32
Orlane	59		Enfasi Hair Care	34		Every Body	35
Orly International	59		Every Body	35		Forever Living	36
Otto Basics	59		For Pet's Sake	36		Home Health Products	40
Parlux Fragrances	59		Home Health Products	40		InterNatural	42
Patricia Allison	59		Image Laboratories	41		Katonah Scentral	45
Paul Mazzotta	59		InterNatural	42		Levlad/Nature's Gate	49
Paul Penders	60		Jason Natural Cosmetics	42		Liberty Natural	49
Perfect Balance	60		John Amico	45		Logona USA	50
Prescriptives	62		J.R. Liggett	45		Lotus Light	50
Prestige Cosmetics	62		Jurlique	45		Natural World	54
Rachel Perry	63		K.B. Products	46		Neways	57
Redken	63		KMS Research	46		NutriBiotic	58
Reviva Labs	64		Lander Company	47		Oxyfresh Worldwide	59
Revlon	64		L'anza	49		Pathmark Stores	59
Royal Labs	64		Levlad/Nature's Gate	49		Shaklee	66
Shaklee	66		Lissée Cosmetics	50		SoapBerry Shop	
Shene Cosmetics	66		Logona USA	50		Company	67
Shivani Ayurvedic			Mastey de Paris	51		Steps in Health	69
Cosmetics	66		Mill Creek	52		Sunrider International	70
SoapBerry Shop			Naturade Cosmetics	53		Sunrise Lane	70
Company	67		Natural Bodycare	54		Thursday Plantation	71
Sombra Cosmetics	67		Nature's Plus	55		Tom's of Maine	71
Spa Natural	69		Nexxus	57		Weleda	75
Studio Magic	69		Paul Mazzotta	59		Wisdom Toothbrush Co.	75
Sunrider International	70		Pure & Basic Products	62			
Tammy Taylor Nails	70		Redken	63			
TauT	70		Reviva Labs	64		**DEODORANT**	
Terressentials	71		Sunshine Natural				
Ultima II	72		Products	70		Almay	12
Ultra Glow	72		Thursday Plantation	71		Aramis	15
Urban Decay	72					Aubrey Organics	17
Warm Earth Cosmetics	75					Bare Escentuals	18
Zia Cosmetics	76						

81

Bath and Body Works	19	
Bath Island	19	
Beauty Naturally	20	
Body Shop	21	
Caswell-Massey	24	
Chanel	25	
Clinique	26	
Creighton's Naturally	28	
Deodorant Stones of America	29	
Desert Essence	30	
Estée Lauder	34	
Every Body	35	
Faith Products	35	
For Pet's Sake	36	
French Transit	37	
Garden Botanika	37	
Hargen Distributing	39	
Jason Natural Cosmetics	42	
Lander Company	47	
Levlad/Nature's Gate	49	
Liz Claiborne	50	
Louise Bianco	50	
Mill Creek	52	
Nature de France	54	
North Country Soap	57	
Pure and Basic Products	62	
Queen Helene	63	
Revlon	64	
Shaklee	66	
Soap Opera	67	
Steps in Health	69	
Sunrise Lane	70	
Terressentials	71	
Tom's of Maine	71	
U.S. Sales Service	72	
Warm Earth Cosmetics	75	
Weleda	75	

ETHNIC PRODUCTS

Almay	12
Aveda	18
Avon	18
Bobbi Brown	21
Citré Shine	25
Clinique	26
M.A.C.	50
Maybelline	51
Nature de France	54

Origins Natural Resources	58
Prescriptives	62
Queen Helene	63
Revlon	64

FEMININE HYGIENE

Amway Corporation	15
CamoCare Camomile	24
Celestial Body	25
Home Health Products	40
InterNatural	42
Jason Natural Cosmetics	42
Lotus Light	50
Natracare	53
Seventh Generation	66
Womankind	75

FRAGRANCES FOR MEN

Abercrombie & Fitch	11
Ahimsa	11
Aloette	12
Amway	15
Ananda Collection	15
Aramis	15
Aromaland	16
Aroma Vera	16
Aubrey Organics	17
Aura Cacia	17
Auroma International	17
Avon	18
Ayurherbal Corporation	18
Bare Escentuals	18
Bath and Body Works	19
BeautiControl	19
Better Botanicals	20
Body Shop	21
Body Time	22
Botanicus Retail	22
Caswell-Massey	24
Chanel	25
Christian Dior	25
Clientele	26
Columbia Cosmetics	26
Common Scents	26
Compar	26
Cosmair	27

Crabtree & Evelyn	28
Crown Royale	28
Davidoff Fragrances	28
Decleor USA	28
Essential Oil Company	34
Essential Products of America	34
Fernand Aubry	36
Finelle Cosmetics	36
Fragrance Impressions	37
Garden Botanika	37
Georgette Klinger	37
Gucci Parfums	39
Hewitt Soap Company	40
Homebody	40
H2O Plus	41
Jessica McClintock	45
Katonah Scentral	45
Kiehl's Since 1851	46
KSA Jojoba	46
Logona USA	50
L'Oréal	50
Lotus Light	50
Marilyn Miglin Institute	51
Mère Cie	51
Natura	53
Natural Science	54
Nectarine	55
No Common Scents	57
Oriflame Corporation	58
Parfums Houbigant Paris	59
Parlux Fragrances	59
Perfect Balance	60
PlantEssence	60
Potions & Lotions	62
Quan Yin Essentials	63
Santa Fe Botanical Fragrances	64
SoapBerry Shop Company	67
Terressentials	71
Warm Earth Cosmetics	75

FRAGRANCES FOR WOMEN

Ahimsa	11
Alexandra Avery	11
Aloette Cosmetics	12
Amway	15

82

Ananda Collection	15	Herb Garden	40	**FURNITURE POLISH**	
Aramis	15	Hewitt Soap Company	40		
Aromaland	16	Homebody	40	Advange	11
Aroma Vera	16	H2O Plus	41	Amazon Premium	
Aubrey Organics	17	Ilona	41	Products	13
Aura Cacia	17	Jessica McClintock	45	Amway	15
Auroma International	17	Katonah Scentral	45	Earth Friendly	30
Avon	18	Kiehl's Since 1851	46	Earthly Matters	32
Ayurherbal Corporation	18	KSA Jojoba	46	Eco Design Company	32
Bare Escentuals	18	LaNatura	47	Golden Pride/Rawleigh	39
Bath and Body Works	19	La Prairie	49	InterNatural	42
BeautiControl Cosmetics	19	Liberty Natural	49	Natural World	54
Bella's Secret Garden	20	Liz Claiborne	50	WiseWays Herbals	75
Belle Star	20	L'Oréal	50		
Better Botanicals	20	Lotus Light	50	**HAIR CARE**	
Beverly Hills Cosmetic		Marilyn Miglin Institute	51		
Group	20	Mère Cie	51	ABBA Products	11
Body Shop	21	Natura	53	Abkit	11
Body Time	22	Natural Bodycare	54	Advange	11
Botanicus Retail	22	Natural Science	54	African Bio-Botanica	11
Caswell-Massey	24	Nectarine	55	Ahimsa	11
Chanel	25	No Common Scents	57	Aloe Up	13
Christian Dior	25	Oriflame Corporation	58	Alvin Last	13
Clarins of Paris	25	Origins Natural		American Formulating	13
Clientele	26	Resources	58	Amitée Cosmetics	13
Clinique	26	Orlane	59	Amway	15
Color Me Beautiful	26	Parfums Houbigant Paris	59	Aramis	15
Columbia Cosmetics	26	Parlux Fragrances	59	Arizona Natural	
Common Scents	26	Patricia Allison	59	Resources	15
Compar	26	Perfect Balance	60	Aroma Vera	16
Compassion Matters	27	PlantEssence	60	Aubrey Organics	17
Cosmair	27	Potions & Lotions	62	Aveda	18
Cosmyl	27	Prescriptives	62	Avon	18
Crabtree & Evelyn	28	Prestige Fragrances	62	Bare Escentuals	18
Crown Royale	28	Pure Touch Therapeutic	63	Basically Natural	18
Decleor USA	28	Quan Yin Essentials	63	Basic Elements	19
Ecco Bella Botanicals	32	Redken	63	Bath and Body Works	19
Essential Aromatics	34	Santa Fe Botanical	64	Bath Island	19
Essential Oil Company	34	Shivani Ayurvedic		Baudelaire	19
Essential Products of		Cosmetics	66	Beauty Naturally	20
America	34	Simple Wisdom	67	Beauty Without Cruelty	20
Estée Lauder	34	Smith & Vandiver	67	Beehive Botanicals	20
Fernand Aubry	36	SoapBerry Shop		Bella's Secret Garden	20
Finelle Cosmetics	36	Company	67	Bio-Tec Cosmetics	21
Forest Essentials	36	Soap Opera	67	Body Shop	21
Fragrance Impressions	37	Spa Natural	69	Body Time	22
Garden Botanika	37	Terra Nova	70	Börlind of Germany	22
Georgette Klinger	37	Terressentials	71	Botanics Skin Care	22
Gryphon Development	39	Tova Corporation	71	Brocato International	22
Gucci Parfums	39	Victoria's Secret	73	Caeran	24
Henri Bendel	40	V'tae Parfum	74		

83

CamoCare Camomile	24	Jason Natural Cosmetics	42	Rainbow Research	63
Carina Supply	24	Jheri Redding	45	Rainforest Company	63
Carlson Laboratories	24	John Amico	45	Redken	63
Caswell-Massey	24	John Paul Mitchell	45	Redmond Products	63
Chuckles	25	JOICO Laboratories	45	Reviva Labs	64
Citré Shine	25	J.R. Liggett	45	Revlon	64
Clientele	26	Jurlique	45	Royal Labs	64
Clinique	26	Katonah Scentral	45	Rusk	64
Columbia Cosmetics	26	K.B. Products	46	Santa Fe Soap Company	65
Compassion Matters	27	Ken Lange No-Thio	46	Scruples	65
Conair	27	Kenra Laboratories	46	Sebastian	65
Creighton's Naturally	28	Kiehl's Since 1851	46	Shikai	66
Decleor USA	28	Kiss My Face	46	Shivani Ayurvedic	
Dep Corporation	29	KMS Research	46	Cosmetics	66
Derma-E	29	KSA Jojoba	46	Simple Wisdom	67
Dermatologic Cosmetic		La Costa Products	46	Smith & Vandiver	67
Laboratories	30	Lander Company	47	SoapBerry Shop	
Desert Essence	30	L'anza	49	Company	67
Dr. Bronner's	30	Life Dynamics	49	Soap Opera	67
Dr. Hauschka	30	Lissée Cosmetics	50	SoRik International	69
Earth Science	32	Logona USA	50	Soya System	69
E. Burnham Cosmetics	32	L'Oréal	50	Spa Natural	69
Ecco Bella Botanicals	32	Lotus Light	50	Steps in Health	69
Edward & Sons Trading	32	M.A.C.	50	Stevens Research	69
Enfasi Hair Care	34	Magick Botanicals	51	Sukesha	69
Espial Corporation	34	Magic of Aloe	51	Sunrider International	70
Essential Aromatics	34	Mastey de Paris	51	Sunrise Lane	70
Every Body	35	Mill Creek	52	Sunshine Natural	
Faith Products	35	Montagne Jeunesse	52	Products	70
Finelle Cosmetics	36	Mountain Ocean	52	Supreme Beauty Products	70
Focus 21 International	36	Naturade Cosmetics	53	Terressentials	71
Forever Living Products	36	Natural Bodycare	54	Thursday Plantation	71
For Pet's Sake	36	Natural World	54	Tisserand Aromatherapy	71
Framesi USA	37	Nature Clean	54	Tom's of Maine	71
Freeman	37	Nature de France	54	Tova Corporation	71
Fruit of the Earth	37	Nature's Plus	55	Trader Joe's	71
Garden Botanika	37	Nectarine	55	Travel Mates America	71
Georgette Klinger	37	Neways	57	Tressa	71
Giovanni Cosmetics	39	Nexxus	57	TRI Hair Care	71
Goldwell Cosmetics	39	Nirvana	57	Von Myering	74
Greenway Products	39	NuSkin International	57	Wachters'	74
Helen Lee Skin Care	40	Oriflame Corporation	58	Weleda	75
Hobé Laboratories	40	Orjene Natural		Wella Corporation	75
Homebody	40	Cosmetics	58	WiseWays Herbals	75
Home Health Products	40	Oxyfresh Worldwide	59	Wysong	76
H2O Plus	41	Paul Mazzotta	59		
Il-Makiage	41	Paul Penders	60		
Ilona	41	Perfect Balance	60	**HAIR COLOR**	
Image Laboratories	41	Potions & Lotions	62		
i natural cosmetics	41	Pure & Basic Products	62	Alvin Last	13
IQ Products Company	42	Queen Helene	63	Avigal Henna	18

Beauty Naturally	20	Auroma International	17	Mia Rose Products	52
Bio-Tec Cosmetics	21	Ayurherbal Corporation	18	Natural Animal Health	53
Body Shop	21	Basically Natural	18	Natural Bodycare	54
Carina Supply	24	Bath and Body Works	19	Natural Chemistry	54
Chuckles	25	Bath Island	19	Natural World	54
Conair	27	Bella's Secret Garden	20	Nature Clean	54
Cosmair	27	Bo-Chem Company	21	Neocare Laboratories	55
Every Body	35	Bon Ami/Faultless Starch	22	Neway	57
Farmavita USA (Chuckles)	35	Botanicus Retail	22	Neways	57
Framesi USA	37	Caeran	24	Nutri-Metics	58
Garnier	37	CHIP Distribution	25	Oxyfresh Worldwide	59
Goldwell Cosmetics	39	Clear Vue Products	26	Planet	60
Il-Makiage	41	Common Scents	26	Pure & Basic Products	62
Image Laboratories	41	Compassionate Consumer	27	Safeway	64
InterNatural	42			SerVaas Laboratories	66
John Amico	45	Compassion Matters	27	Seventh Generation	66
JOICO Laboratories	45	Cot 'n Wash	27	Shadow Lake	66
Katonah Scentral	45	Country Save	27	Shaklee	66
L'anza	49	Crown Royale	28	Simple Wisdom	67
Logona USA	50	DeSoto	30	Sinclair & Valentine	67
L'Oréal	50	Earth Friendly	30	Smith & Vandiver	67
Mastey de Paris	51	Earthly Matters	32	Stanhome	69
Nexxus	57	Ecco Bella Botanicals	32	Steps in Health	69
Paul Mazzotta	59	Ecover	32	Sunrider International	70
Paul Penders	60	Edward & Sons Trading	32	Sunrise Lane	70
Rainbow Research	63	Espial Corporation	34	Terressentials	71
Redken	63	Evans International	35	Trader Joe's	71
Revlon	64	Faultless Starch	35	Vapor Products	73
Scruples	65	Food Lion	36	Vermont Soapworks	73
Sebastian	65	Forever Living	36	V'tae Parfum	74
Sukesha	69	For Pet's Sake	36		
Sunrise Lane	70	Frontier Natural Products	37		
Terressentials	71	Golden Pride/Rawleigh	39	**HYPO-ALLERGENIC SKIN**	
Tish & Snooky's	71	Greenway Products	39	**CARE**	
Von Myering	74	Harvey Universal	39		
Wella Corporation	75	h.e.r.c. Consumer Products	40	Alexandra Avery	11
				Almay	12
		Home Health Products	40	Aloe Up	13
HOUSEHOLD PRODUCTS		Home Service Products	41	Arizona Natural Resources	15
		Huish Detergents	41		
ABEnterprises	11	Innovative Formulations	41	Aubrey Organics	17
Abkit	11	J.C. Garet	42	Avon	18
Advanage	11	Jurlique	45	Bare Escentuals	18
Allens Naturally	12	Kleen Brite	46	Basically Natural	18
Amazon Premium Products	13	Liberty Natural	49	Bath and Body Works	19
American Formulating	13	Life Tree Products	49	Baudelaire	19
America's Finest	13	Lightning Products	49	BeautiControl Cosmetics	19
Amway	15	Lime-O-Sol Company	49	Beauty Without Cruelty	20
Ananda Collection	15	Marcal Paper Mills	51	Bella's Secret Garden	20
Astonish Industries	16	Marché Image	51	Botan Corporation	22
Aubrey Organics	17	Mère Cie	51	Botanics Skin Care	22

Botanicus Retail	22	North Country Soap	57	**LAUNDRY DETERGENT**	
Caeran	24	Nutri-Cell	58		
Carina Supply	24	Oriflame Corporation	58	Allens Naturally	12
Celestial Body	25	Orlane	59	Amway	15
Christine Valmy	25	Paul Mazzotta	59	Astonish Industries	16
Clarins of Paris	25	Paul Penders	60	Basically Natural	18
Clientele	26	Perfect Balance	60	Caeran	24
Color My Image	26	Pharmagel	60	Country Save	27
Crème de la Terre	28	Potions & Lotions	62	Earth Friendly	30
Decleor USA	28	Pure & Basic Products	62	Earthly Matters	32
Derma-E	29	Rainbow Research	63	Eco Design Company	32
Dermatologic Cosmetic		Redken	63	Faith Products	35
Laboratories	30	Reviva Labs	64	Golden Pride/Rawleigh	39
Desert Naturels	30	Royal Labs	64	Home Service Products	41
E. Burnham Cosmetics	32	Shaklee	66	InterNatural	42
Ecco Bella Botanicals	32	Shirley Price	66	James Austin Company	42
Eco Design Company	32	SoapBerry Shop		Kleen Brite Laboratories	46
Elizabeth Grady	34	Company	67	Life Tree Products	49
Elizabeth Van Buren	34	Spa Natural	69	Natural World	54
Essential Products of		Studio Magic	69	Nature Clean	54
America	34	Sunrise Lane	70	Oxyfresh Worldwide	59
European Gold	35	Tammy Taylor Nails	70	Planet	60
Face Food Shoppe	35	Thursday Plantation	71	Seventh Generation	66
Faces by Gustavo	35	Truly Moist	72	Shaklee	66
Garden Botanika	37	Tyra Skin Care	72	Sunrise Lane	70
Greenway Products	39	Wellington	75	Wachters'	74
Helen Lee Skin Care	40			Whip-It Products	75
Homebody	40				
Ida Grae	41	**INSECT REPELLANT/**			
Il-Makiage	41	**TREATMENT**		**LAUNDRY DETERGENT**	
i natural cosmetics	41			**FOR FINE WASHABLES**	
Jason Natural Cosmetics	42	Aromaland	16		
Jeanne Rose		Aubrey Organics	17	Cot 'n Wash	27
Aromatherapy	42	Avon	18	Forever New	
Kimberly Sayer	46	Basically Natural	18	International	36
KSA Jojoba	46	Bath and Body Works	19		
La Crista	47	Bug Off	22	**MAKEUP BRUSH (VEGAN)**	
Levlad/Nature's Gate	49	Compassion Matters	27		
Life Dynamics	49	Essential Oil Company	34	Origins	58
Logona USA	50	Green Ban	39		
L'Oréal	50	Herbal Products	40	**NAIL CARE**	
Louise Bianco	50	Herb Garden	40		
M.A.C.	50	Home Health Products	40	Aloette Cosmetics	12
Micro Balanced Products	52	InterNatural	42	Amoresse Laboratories	15
Mira Linder Spa	52	IQ Products	42	Andrea International	15
Narwhale of High Tor	53	Jason Natural Cosmetics	42	Ardell International	15
Naturade Cosmetics	53	Lotus Light	50	Avon	18
Natural Science	54	North Country Soap	57	Bare Escentuals	18
Natural World	54	SunFeather Natural Soap	70	Bath and Body Works	19
Neocare Laboratories	55	Terressentials	71		
Neways	57	V'tae Parfum	74		
		WiseWays Herbals	75		

Bath Island	19		OFFICE SUPPLIES			RAZORS		
BeautiControl	19							
Body Shop	21		Berol	20		American Safety Razor	13	
Chanel	25		Citius USA	25		Aramis	15	
Christian Dior	25		D.R.P.C.	30		Body Shop	21	
Clarins of Paris	25		Eberhard Faber	32		Compassion Matters	27	
Clinique Laboratories	26		Evans International	35		Crabtree & Evelyn	28	
Color My Image	26		International Rotex	42		Norelco	57	
Columbia Cosmetics	26		Pilot	60		Pathmark Stores	59	
Cosmair	27		Sanford	64		USA King's Crossing	72	
Cosmyl	27		Staedtler	69				
Decleor USA	28							
Dermatologic Cosmetic						SHAVING SUPPLY		
Laboratories	30		PAINT					
Diamond Brands	30					ABBA Products	11	
Elizabeth Grady	34		American Formulating	13		Advanage	11	
Essential Aromatics	34		Eco Design Company	32		Alba Botanica	11	
Estée Lauder	34		Innovative Formulations	41		Alexandra Avery	11	
Every Body	35					Alvin Last	13	
Fernand Aubry	36					American Safety Razor	13	
For Pet's Sake	36		PERMANENTS			Aramis	15	
Garden Botanika	37					Aubrey Organics	17	
Georgette Klinger	37		ABBA Products	11		Bare Escentuals	18	
Hard Candy	39		Beauty Naturally	20		Bath and Body Works	19	
Home Health Products	40		Bio-Tec Cosmetics	21		Bath Island	19	
H2O Plus	41		Brocato International	22		Body Encounters	21	
Il-Makiage	41		Carina Supply	24		Bodyography	21	
Ilona	41		Chuckles	25		Body Shop	21	
InterNatural	42		Conair	27		Body Time	22	
Jason Natural Cosmetics	42		Framesi USA	37		Botan Corporation	22	
La Costa Products	46		Image Laboratories	41		Caswell-Massey	24	
Lee Pharmaceuticals	49		Jheri Redding	45		Celestial Body	25	
L'Oréal	50		John Amico	45		Christine Valmy	25	
M.A.C.	50		John Paul Mitchell	45		Clinique Laboratories	26	
Mira Linder Spa	52		JOICO Laboratories	45		Comfort Manufacturing	26	
Montagne Jeunesse	52		Ken Lange No-Thio	46		Common Scents	26	
Nature's Plus	55		KMS Research	46		Crabtree & Evelyn	28	
Neways	57		L'anza	49		Creighton's Naturally	28	
OPI Products	58		L'Oréal	50		Crown Royale	28	
Orly International	59		Mastey de Paris	51		Decleor USA	28	
Prestige Cosmetics	62		Nexxus	57		Earth Science	32	
Revlon	64		Paul Mazzotta	59		Ecco Bella Botanicals	32	
Shene Cosmetics	66		Redken	63		Eco Design Company	32	
SoapBerry Shop Company	67		Scruples	65		Estée Lauder	34	
Sunrider International	70		Soya System	69		Every Body	35	
Tammy Taylor Nails	70		Stevens Research	69		Face Food Shoppe	35	
Tish & Snooky's	71		Sunrise Lane	70		Faith Products	35	
Urban Decay	72		Von Myering	74		Garden Botanika	37	
			Wella Corporation	75		Georgette Klinger	37	
						Greenway Products	39	
						Gucci Parfums	39	

Homebody Perfumoils	40	Aloegen Natural	12	Citré Shine	25
H2O Plus	41	Aloette	12	Clarins of Paris	25
i natural cosmetics	41	Aloe Up	13	Clientele	26
Jessica McClintock	45	Aloe Vera of America	13	Clinique	26
John Amico	45	Alvin Last	13	Color Me Beautiful	26
Katonah Scentral	45	American International	13	Color My Image	26
Kiss My Face	46	Amway	15	Columbia Cosmetics	26
La Costa Products	46	Ancient Formulas	15	Comfort Manufacturing	26
Lander Company	47	Andrea International	15	Common Scents	26
Liz Claiborne Cosmetics	50	Aramis	15	Compassion Matters	27
Logona USA	50	Arbonne International	15	Concept Now Cosmetics	27
Magic of Aloe	51	Ardell International	15	Cosmyl	27
Mill Creek	52	Arizona Natural		Country Comfort	27
Natural (Surrey)	53	Resources	15	Creighton's Naturally	28
Nature de France	54	Aroma Vera	16	Crème de la Terre	28
Nectarine	55	Aubrey Organics	17	Decleor USA	28
Neways	57	Aunt Bee's	17	Derma-E	29
Origins	58	Aura Cacia	17	Dermalogica	29
Orjene Natural Cosmetics	58	Auromère Ayurvedic		Dermatologic Cosmetic	
Paul Penders	60	Imports	18	Laboratories	30
Potions & Lotions	62	Aveda	18	Desert Essence	30
Pure & Basic Products	62	Avon	18	Desert Naturels	30
Queen Helene	63	Bare Escentuals	18	Dr. Hauschka	30
Redken	63	Basically Natural	18	Earth Science	32
Reviva Labs	64	Basic Elements	19	Earth Solutions	32
Royal Labs	64	Bath and Body Works	19	E. Burnham Cosmetics	32
Shaklee	66	Bath Island	19	Ecco Bella Botanicals	32
Smith & Vandiver	67	BeautiControl	19	Elizabeth Grady	34
SoapBerry Shop		Beauty Without Cruelty	20	Elizabeth Van Buren	34
Company	67	Beehive Botanicals	20	Espial Corporation	34
Sunrider International	70	Beiersdorf	20	Essential Aromatics	34
Sunrise Lane	70	Bella's Secret Garden	20	Essential Products of	
Surrey	70	Biogime	21	America	34
Terra Nova	70	Bio-Tec Cosmetics	21	Estée Lauder	34
Terressentials	71	Body Encounters	21	European Gold	35
Tom's of Maine	71	Body Shop	21	EuroZen	35
USA Kings Crossing	72	Body Time	22	Face Food Shoppe	35
Wellington Labs	75	Bonne Bell	22	Faces by Gustavo	35
Wysong Corporation	76	Botan Corporation	22	Facets/Crystalline	35
		Botanicus Retail	22	Faith Products	35
		Bronzo Sensualé	22	Fernand Aubry	36
SKIN CARE		California SunCare	24	Finelle Cosmetics	36
		CamoCare Camomile	24	Forest Essentials	36
ABBA Products	11	Carina Supply	24	Forever Living	36
Abkit	11	Carlson Laboratories	24	For Pet's Sake	36
Abra Therapeutics	11	Caswell-Massey	24	Freeman	37
Adrien Arpel	11	Celestial Body	25	Fruit of the Earth	37
African Bio-Botanica	11	Chanel	25	Garden Botanika	37
Alba Botanica	11	Chatoyant Pearl	25	Georgette Klinger	37
Alexandra Avery	11	Christian Dior	25	Gigi Laboratories	37
Almay	12	Christine Valmy	25	Greenway Products	39

Gucci Parfums	39	
Helen Lee Skin Care	40	
Herb Garden	40	
Hobé Laboratories	40	
Homebody (Perfumoils)	40	
Home Health Products	40	
House of Cheriss	41	
H2O Plus	41	
Ida Grae	41	
Il-Makiage	41	
i natural cosmetics	41	
InterNatural	42	
Jacki's Magic Lotion	42	
Jason Natural Cosmetics	42	
Jeanne Rose Aromatherapy	42	
Jennifer Tara	45	
Joe Blasco Cosmetics	45	
John Paul Mitchell	45	
JOICO Laboratories	45	
Kenra Laboratories	46	
Kiehl's Since 1851	46	
Kimberly Sayer	46	
Kiss My Face	46	
KSA Jojoba	46	
La Costa Products	46	
La Crista	47	
LaNatura	47	
Lander Company	47	
La Prairie	49	
Levlad/Nature's Gate	49	
Liberty Natural	49	
Life Dynamics	49	
Lily of Colorado	49	
Lissée Cosmetics	50	
Logona USA	50	
L'Oréal	50	
Lotus Light	50	
Louise Bianco	50	
M.A.C.	50	
Magick Botanicals	51	
Magic of Aloe	51	
Marché Image	51	
Marilyn Miglin Institute	51	
Mastey de Paris	51	
Merle Norman	52	
Michelle Lazar	52	
Micro Balanced Products	52	
Mill Creek	52	
Mira Linder Spa	52
Montagne Jeunesse	52
Narwhale of High Tor	53
Naturade Cosmetics	53
Natural Animal Health Products	53
Natural Bodycare	54
Natural Science	54
Natural World	54
Nature de France	54
Nature's Plus	55
Nectarine	55
Neocare Laboratories	55
Neways	57
New Chapter Extracts	57
Nirvana	57
Nordstrom	57
North Country Soap	57
NuSkin International	57
Nutri-Cell	58
Ohio Hempery	58
Oriflame Corporation	58
Origins	58
Orjene Natural Cosmetics	58
Orly International	59
Oxyfresh Worldwide	59
Parfums Houbigant Paris	59
Patricia Allison	59
Paul Mazzotta	59
Paul Penders	60
Perfect Balance	60
Pharmagel	60
PlantEssence	60
Potions & Lotions	62
Prescription Plus	62
Prescriptives	62
Principal Secret	62
Pure & Basic Products	62
Quan Yin Essentials	63
Queen Helene	63
Rachel Perry	63
Rainbow Research	63
Redken	63
Reviva Labs	64
Revlon	64
Royal Labs	64
San Francisco Soap	64
Sebastian	66
Shaklee	66
Shikai	66

Shirley Price	66
Shivani Ayurvedic Cosmetics	66
Simple Wisdom	67
Sinclair & Valentine	67
Smith & Vandiver	67
SoapBerry Shop Company	67
Sombra Cosmetics	67
Spa Natural	69
Steps in Health	69
Studio Magic	69
Sunrider International	70
Sunrise Lane	70
Tammy Taylor Nails	70
TauT	70
Terra Nova	70
Terressentials	71
Thursday Plantation	71
Tisserand Aromatherapy	71
Tova Corporation	71
Truly Moist	72
Tyra Skin Care	72
USA King's Crossing	72
Victoria's Secret	73
Von Myering	74
Wala-Heilmittel	75
Weleda	75
Wellington	75
WiseWays Herbals	75
Zia Cosmetics	76

SUN CARE/TANNING

Abra Therapeutics	11
Alba Botanica	11
Alexandra Avery	11
Almay	12
Aloette	12
Aloe Up	13
Amway	15
Aramis	15
Arizona Natural Resources	15
Aubrey Organics	17
Autumn-Harp	18
Avon	18
Basically Natural	18
Bath and Body Works	19
Bath Island	19

BeautiControl	19	Liberty Natural	49	**THEATRICAL MAKEUP**	
Beauty Without Cruelty		Lissée Cosmetics	50		
Cosmetics	20	Logona USA	50	Cinema Secrets	25
Biogime	21	Louise Bianco	50	Clientele	26
Body Encounters	21	Magic of Aloe	51	Color My Image	26
Body Shop	21	Mastey de Paris	51	Joe Blasco Cosmetics	45
Body Time	22	Micro Balanced		M.A.C.	50
Bonne Bell	22	Products	52	Mehron	51
Bronzo Sensualé	22	Mill Creek	52	Sombra Cosmetics	67
Chanel	25	Narwhale of High Tor	53	Studio Magic	69
Christine Valmy	25	Natural Bodycare	54	TauT	70
Clarins of Paris	25	Natural Science	54	Ultra Glow	72
Clientele	26	Natural World	54	Urban Decay	72
Clinique	26	Neways	57		
Color Me Beautiful	26	North Country Soap	57		
Color My Image	26	NuSkin International	57	**TOILETRIES/PERSONAL**	
Columbia Cosmetics	26	Nutri-Cell	58	**CARE**	
Compassion Matters	27	Oriflame Corporation	58		
Concept Now Cosmetics	27	Origins	58	ABEnterprises	11
Crème de la Terre	28	Orjene Natural		Abercrombie & Fitch	11
Decleor USA	28	Cosmetics	58	Abkit	11
Derma-E	29	Orlane	59	Alba Botanica	11
Dermalogica	29	Patricia Allison	59	Alexandra Avery	11
Dermatologic Cosmetic		Paul Mazzotta	59	Aloette	12
Laboratories	30	Perfect Balance	60	Aloe Up	13
Earth Science	32	Pharmagel	60	Aloe Vera of America	13
Elizabeth Grady	34	Potions & Lotions	62	Alvin Last	13
Estée Lauder	34	Prescription Plus	62	American International	13
European Gold	35	Prescriptives	62	American Safety Razor	13
Every Body	35	Rachel Perry	63	Amway	15
Faces by Gustavo	35	Reviva Labs	64	Aramis	15
Faith Products	35	Royal Labs	64	Arizona Natural	
Finelle Cosmetics	36	Shaklee	66	Resources	15
Forest Essentials	36	Smith & Vandiver	67	Aroma Vera	16
Forever Living	36	SoapBerry Shop		Aubrey Organics	17
Freeman	37	Company	67	Aura Cacia	17
Fruit of the Earth	37	SoRik International	69	Auroma International	17
Garden Botanika	37	Spa Natural	69	Auromère Ayurvedic	
Georgette Klinger	37	Studio Magic	69	Imports	18
Hawaiian Resources	40	Sunrider International	70	Avon	18
H2O Plus	41	Sunrise Lane	70	Ayurherbal Corporation	18
i natural cosmetics	41	Tammy Taylor Nails	70	Bare Escentuals	18
InterNatural	42	TauT	70	Basically Natural	18
Jason Natural Cosmetics	42	Thursday Plantation	71	Bath Island	19
John Paul Mitchell	45	Tropix Suncare	72	Baudelaire	19
Jurlique	45	Tyra Skin Care	72	Beehive Botanicals	20
Kiss My Face	46	Ultra Glow	72	Bella's Secret Garden	20
La Costa Products	46	Victoria's Secret	73	Belle Star	20
Lancôme	47	Wysong	76	Better Botanicals	20
La Prairie	49	Zia Cosmetics	76	Beverly Hills Cold Wax	20
Levlad/Nature's Gate	49			Biogime	21

Biokosma	21	Eva Jon Cosmetics	35	Naturade Cosmetics	53
Bio Pac	21	Every Body	35	Natural (Surrey)	53
Bio-Tec Cosmetics	21	Face Food Shoppe	35	Natural World	54
Body Encounters	21	Faces by Gustavo	35	Nature de France	54
Body Shop	21	Fernand Aubry	36	Nature's Plus	55
Body Time	22	Finelle Cosmetics	36	Nectarine	55
Börlind of Germany	22	Forest Essentials	36	Neways	57
Botan Corporation	22	Forever Living	36	Nexxus	57
Botanicus Retail	22	For Pet's Sake	36	North Country Soap	57
Caeran	24	Free Spirit Enterprises	37	NuSkin International	57
CamoCare Camomile	24	Frontier Natural Products	37	NutriBiotic	58
Carlson Laboratories	24	Garden Botanika	37	Nutri-Metics	58
Caswell-Massey	24	Georgette Klinger	37	Oliva	58
Celestial Body	25	Greenway Products	39	Oriflame Corporation	58
Chanel	25	Gryphon Development	39	Origins Natural	
Chatoyant Pearl	25	Gucci Parfums	39	Resources	58
Christian Dior	25	Helen Lee Skin Care	40	Orjene Natural	
Christine Valmy	25	Hewitt Soap Company	40	Cosmetics	58
Clarins of Paris	25	Homebody	40	Oxyfresh Worldwide	59
Clientele	26	Home Health Products	40	Pacific Scents	59
Clinique	26	H2O Plus	41	Parfums Houbigant Paris	59
Color My Image	26	i natural cosmetics	41	Paul Mazzotta	59
Common Scents	26	InterNatural	42	Paul Penders	60
Compar	26	Jason Natural Cosmetics	42	PlantEssence	60
Compassionate		Jeanne Rose		Potions & Lotions	62
Consumer	27	Aromatherapy	42	Prescriptives	62
Compassionate		Jessica McClintock	45	Pure & Basic Products	62
Cosmetics	27	Jheri Redding	45	Quan Yin Essentials	63
Compassion Matters	27	John Amico	45	Queen Helene	63
Conair	27	JOICO Laboratories	45	Rainbow Research	63
Cosmyl	27	Jurlique	45	Rainforest Company	63
Crabtree & Evelyn	28	Katonah Scentral	45	Redken	63
Creighton's Naturally	28	Kimberly Sayer	46	Reviva Labs	64
Crème de la Terre	28	Kiss My Face	46	Revlon	64
Crown Royale	28	KSA Jojoba	46	Royal Labs	64
Decleor USA	28	La Costa Products	46	Safeway	64
Dep Corporation	29	LaNatura	47	San Francisco Soap	64
Derma-E	29	Levlad/Nature's Gate	49	Shadow Lake	66
Dermatologic Cosmetic		Liberty Natural	49	Shaklee	66
Laboratories	30	Life Dynamics	49	Shene Cosmetics	66
Desert Essence	30	Liz Claiborne	50	Shivani Ayurvedic	
Dr. Bronner's	30	Logona USA	50	Cosmetics	66
Earth Science	32	L'Oréal	50	Simple Wisdom	67
Earth Solutions	32	Louise Bianco	50	Sinclair & Valentine	67
Elizabeth Grady	34	Magick Botanicals	51	Smith & Vandiver	67
Enfasi Hair Care	34	Magic of Aloe	51	SoapBerry Shop	
Epilady International	34	Mastey de Paris	51	Company	67
Espial Corporation	34	Micro Balanced		SoRik International	69
Essential Products of		Products	52	Spa Natural	69
America	34	Montagne Jeunesse	52	Spanish Bath	69
Estée Lauder	34	Mountain Ocean	52	Steps in Health	69

Sunrider International	70	
Surrey	70	
Tammy Taylor Nails	70	
TauT	70	
Terra Nova	70	
Thursday Plantation	71	
Tisserand Aromatherapy	71	
Tom's of Maine	71	
Trader Joe's	71	
Travel Mates America	71	
Upper Canada Soap	72	
Vermont Soapworks	73	
Victoria's Secret	73	
Virginia Soap	73	
V'tae Parfum	74	
Wachters'	74	
Wala-Heilmittel	75	
Warm Earth Cosmetics	75	
Weleda	75	
Wellington	75	
Wysong Corporation	76	

TOOTHBRUSHES

Bath Island	19
Body Shop	21
Caswell-Massey	24
Compassion Matters	27
Crabtree & Evelyn	28

Dep Corporation	29
Eco Design Company	32
H2O Plus	41
Katonah Scentral	45
Liberty Natural	49
Lotus Light	50
Oxyfresh Worldwide	59
Pathmark Stores	59
Potions & Lotions	62
Safeway	64
SoapBerry Shop Company	67
Soap Opera	67
Wisdom Toothbrush	75

VITAMINS/HERBS

Abra Therapeutics	11
Amway	15
Apothecary Shoppe	15
Auromère Ayurvedic	18
Ayurveda Holistic	18
Beehive Botanicals	20
Better Botanicals	20
Bronson Pharmaceuticals	22
Caeran	24
Clientele	26
Dr. Goodpet	30
Earth Science	32

For Pet's Sake	36
Freeda Vitamins	37
Frontier Natural Products	37
Golden Pride/Rawleigh	39
Helen Lee Skin Care	40
Herbal Products	40
Herb Garden	40
Home Health Products	40
International Vitamin	42
InterNatural	42
Jeanne Rose Aromatherapy	42
Lotus Light	50
Michael's Naturopathic Programs	52
Natural World	54
Nexxus	57
Nutrina Company	58
Oriflame Corporation	58
Oxyfresh Worldwide	59
Pathmark Stores	59
Solgar Vitamin	67
Steps in Health	69
Studio Magic	69
Sunrider International	70
Terressentials	71
The Ultimate Life	72
Wachters'	74
Wysong	76

New Vegetarians Need:

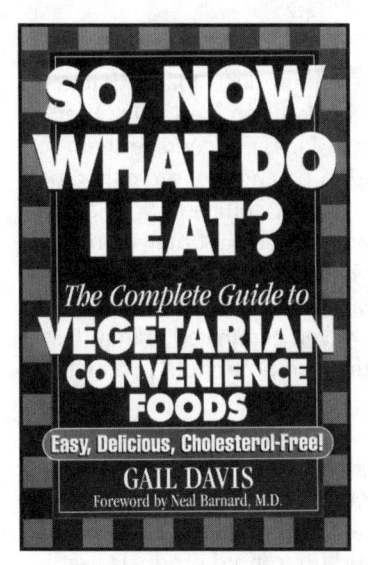

SO, NOW WHAT DO I EAT?

The Complete Guide to Vegetarian Convenience Foods **by Gail Davis**

Millions of Americans are making the switch to an animal-friendly, meat-free diet. But when you toss out the burgers and chicken fajitas, what do you put on your plate instead? Gail Davis' new book answers that question–and more. Focusing on exploration, not deprivation, this wonderful resource will help you discover the incredible range of meat-free foods awaiting you at your local supermarket or health food store– everything from meatless "meats" like veggie burgers and sandwich slices to milk and cheese substitutes, frozen entrées, delicious vegan desserts, and even veggie foods for Fido. If you're already a vegetarian, give this book to friends to show them just how easy ethical eating can be!

To order, send a $15.95 check or money order (postage included) to: PETA Merchandise, 501 Front St., Norfolk, VA 23510.

> "Gail Davis has compiled a comprehensive collection of vegetarian food sources for people on the go. Choosing Earth-friendly, creature-friendly, and health-friendly foods is a positive step each of us can take for the future of life on Earth."
> – John Robbins, author of *Diet for a New America*

PeTA People for the Ethical Treatment of Animals
501 Front St., Norfolk, VA 23510 • 757-622-PETA • www.peta-online.org

Companies That Test on Animals

Why Are These Companies Included on the "Do Test" List?

The following companies manufacture products that <u>ARE</u> tested on animals. Those marked with a check (✓) are presently observing a moratorium on animal testing. Please encourage them to announce a permanent ban. Listed in parentheses are either examples of products manufactured by that company or, if applicable, its parent company. Companies on this list may manufacture individual lines of products without animal testing (e.g., Del Laboratories claims its Naturistics and Natural Glow lines are not animal-tested). They have not, however, eliminated animal testing on their entire line of cosmetics and household products.

Similarly, companies on this list may make some products, such as pharmaceuticals, that are required by law to be tested on animals. However, the reason for these companies' inclusion is not the <u>required</u> animal testing that they conduct, but rather the animal testing of personal care and household products that is <u>not</u> required by law.

What Can Be Done About Animal Tests Required by Law?

Although animal testing of certain pharmaceuticals and chemicals is still mandated by law, the same arguments against using animals in cosmetics testing are valid when applied to the pharmaceutical and chemical industries. These industries are regulated by the Food and Drug Administration and the Environmental Protection Agency, respectively, and animal tests for pharmaceuticals and chemicals are now required by law—laws that were developed haphazardly in the 1920s. We know that non-animal test methods exist <u>right now</u> and that these tests are more accurate in predicting toxicity than are crude, cruel tests on animals. It is the responsibility of the companies that kill animals in order to bring their products to market to convince the regulatory agencies that there is a better way to determine product safety. Companies resist progress because the crude nature of animal tests allows them to market many products that might be determined too toxic if cell culture tests were used. Let companies know how you feel about this.

Alberto-Culver (Tresemmé, Sally Beauty Supply, Alberto V05, TCB Naturals)
2525 W. Armitage Ave.
Melrose Park, IL 60160
708-450-3000
www.alberto.com

Allergan, Inc.
2525 Dupont Dr.
P.O. Box 19534
Irvine, CA 92612
714-752-4500
800-347-4500
corpinfo@allergan.com

Arm & Hammer (Church & Dwight)
P.O. Box 1625
Horsham, PA 19044-6625
609-683-5900
800-524-1328
www.armhammer.com

Bausch & Lomb (Clear Choice)
1 Bausch & Lomb Place
Rochester, NY 14604-2701
716-338-6000
800-344-8815
www.bausch.com

Benckiser (Coty, Lancaster, Jovan)
237 Park Ave., 19th Fl.
New York, NY 10017-3142
212-850-2300
attmail@cotyusa.com

✓ Bic Corporation
500 Bic Dr.
Milford, CT 06460
203-783-2000

Block Drug Co., Inc. (Polident, Sensodyne, Tegrin, Lava, Carpet Fres
257 Cornelison Ave.
Jersey City, NJ 07302
201-434-3000
800-365-6500

Boyle-Midway (Reckitt & Colman)
2 Wickman Rd.
Toronto, ON M8Z 5M5
Canada
416-255-2300

✓ Braun (Gillette Company)
400 Unicorn Park Dr.
Woburn, MA 01801
800-272-8611
braun_usa@braun.de

Bristol-Myers Squibb Co. (Clairol, Ban Roll-On, Keri, Final Net)
345 Park Ave.
New York, NY 10154-0037
212-546-4000
www.bms.com

Calvin Klein (Unilever)
725 Fifth Ave.
New York, NY 10022-2519
212-759-8888
800-745-9696
www.unilever.com

Carter-Wallace (Arrid, Lady's Choice, Nair, Pearl Drops)
1345 Ave. of the Americas
New York, NY 10105-0021
212-339-5000

Chesebrough-Ponds (Fabergé, Cutex, Vaseline)
800 Sylvan Ave.
Englewood Cliffs, NJ 07632
800-243-5804

Church & Dwight (Arm & Hammer)
P.O. Box 1625
Horsham, PA 19044-6625
609-683-5900
800-524-1328
www.armhammer.com

Clairol, Inc. (Bristol-Myers Squibb)
40 W. 57th St., 23rd fl.
New York, NY 10019
212-541-2740
800-223-5800
www.bms.com

Clorox (Pine-Sol, S.O.S., Tilex, ArmorAll)
1221 Broadway
Oakland, CA 94612
510-271-7000
800-227-1860
www.clorox.com

Colgate-Palmolive Co. (Palmolive, Ajax, Fab, Speed Stick, Mennen, SoftSoap)
300 Park Ave.
New York, NY 10022
212-310-2000
800-221-4607
www.colgate.com

Coty (Benckiser)
237 Park Ave., 19th Fl.
New York, NY 10017-3142
212-850-2300
www.cotyusainc.com

Cover Girl (Procter & Gamble)
One Procter & Gamble Plaza
Cincinnati, OH 45202
513-983-1100
800-543-1745
www.covergirl.com

Dana Perfumes (Alyssa Ashley)
470 Oak Hill Rd.
Mountain Top, PA 18707
800-822-8547
www.beautyspot.com

Del Laboratories (Flame Glow, Commerce Drug, Sally Hansen)
565 Broad Hollow Rd.
Farmingdale, NY 11735
516-293-7070
800-645-9888
www.dellabs.com

✓ Dial Corporation (Purex, Renuzit)
15101 N. Scottsdale Rd.
Suite 5028
Scottsdale, AZ 85254-2199
602-207-1800
800-528-0849
www.dialcorp.com

95

DowBrands (Glass Plus, Fantastik, Vivid)
P.O. Box 68511
Indianapolis, IN 46268
317-873-7000
www.dowclean.com

Drackett Products Co. (S.C. Johnson & Son)
1525 Howe St.
Racine, WI 53403
414-631-2000
800-558-5252
www.scjohnsonwax.com

Elizabeth Arden (Unilever)
390 Park Ave.
New York, NY 10022
212-888-1260
800-745-9696
www.unilever.com

Erno Laszlo
89 Park View Ave.
W. Harrison, NY 10604
800-511-7364

✓ **Gillette Co. (Liquid Paper, Flair, Braun, Duracell)**
Prudential Tower Bldg.
Boston, MA 02199
617-421-7000
800-872-7202
www.gillette.com

Givaudan-Roure
1775 Windsor Rd.
Teaneck, NJ 07666
201-833-2300

Helene Curtis Industries (Finesse, Unilever, Suave)
800 Sylvan Ave.
Englewood Cliffs, NJ 07632
800-621-2013
www.unilever.com

Jhirmack (Playtex)
300 Nyala Farms Rd.
Westport, CT 06880
203-341-4000

Johnson & Johnson (Neutrogena)
1 Johnson & Johnson Plaza
New Brunswick, NJ 08933
908-524-0400
www.jnj.com

Kimberly-Clark Corp. (Kleenex, Scott Paper, Huggies)
P.O. Box 619100
Dallas, TX 75261-9100
800-544-1847
www.kimberly-clark.com

Lamaur
5601 E. River Rd.
Fridley, MN 55432
612-571-1234

Lever Bros. (Unilever)
800 Sylvan Ave.
Englewood Cliffs, NJ 07632
212-888-1260
800-598-1223
www.unilever.com

✓ **Mary Kay Cosmetics**
3219 McKinney Ave.
Dallas, TX 75204
214-754-6000
800-201-1362
www.marykay.com

Max Factor (Procter & Gamble)
One Procter & Gamble Plaza
Cincinnati, OH 45202
513-983-1100
800-543-1745
www.pg.com/info

Mead
Courthouse Plaza N.E.
Dayton, OH 45463
937-495-3312
www.mead.com

Melaleuca, Inc.
3910 S. Yellowstone Hwy.
Idaho Falls, ID 83402-6003
208-522-0700

Mennen Co. (Colgate-Palmolive)
E. Hanover Ave.
Morristown, NJ 07962
201-631-9000
www.colgate.com

Neoteric Cosmetics
4880 Havana St.
Denver, CO 80239-0019
303-373-4860

Noxell (Procter & Gamble)
11050 York Rd.
Hunt Valley, MD 21030-2098
410-785-7300
800-572-3282
www.pg.com

Olay Co./Oil of Olay (Procter & Gamble)
P.O. Box 599
Cincinnati, OH 45201
800-543-1745
www.pg.com

✓ **Oral-B (Gillette Company)**
1 Lagoon Dr.
Redwood City, CA 94065-1561
415-598-5000
www.oralb.com

Pantene (Procter & Gamble)
Procter & Gamble Plaza
Cincinnati, OH 45202
800-945-7768
www.pg.com

Parfums International (White Shoulders)
1345 Ave. of the Americas
New York, NY 10105
212-261-1000

✓ **Parker Pens (Gillette Company)**
P.O. Box 5100
Janesville, WI 53547-5100
608-755-7000
braun_usa@braun.de

Perrigo
117 Water St.
Allegan, MI 49010
616-673-8451
800-253-3606
www.perrigo.com

Pfizer, Inc. (Bain de Soleil, Plax, Visine, Desitin, BenGay)
235 E. 42nd St.
New York, NY 10017-5755
212-573-2323
www.pfizer.com

Playtex Products, Inc. (Banana Boat, Woolite, Jhirmack)
300 Nyala Farms Rd.
Westport, CT 06880
203-341-4000
www.playtex.com

Procter & Gamble Co. (Crest, Tide, Cover Girl, Max Factor, Giorgio)
One Procter & Gamble Plaza
Cincinnati, OH 45202
513-983-1100
800-543-1745
www.pg.com/info

Reckitt & Colman (Lysol, Mop & Glo)
1655 Valley Rd.
Wayne, NJ 07474-0945
201-633-6700
800-232-9665

Richardson-Vicks (Procter & Gamble)
One Procter & Gamble Plaza
Cincinnati, OH 45202
513-983-1100
800-543-1745
www.pg.com/info

Sally Hansen (Del Laboratories)
565 Broad Hollow Rd.
Farmingdale, NY 11735
516-293-7070
800-645-9888
www.dellabs.com

Sanofi (Oscar de la Renta, Yves Saint Laurent)
90 Park Ave., 24th Fl.
New York, NY 10016
212-551-4757

Schering-Plough (Coppertone)
1 Giralda Farms
Madison, NJ 07940-1000
201-822-7000
800-842-4090
www.sch-plough.com

Schick (Warner-Lambert)
201 Tabor Rd.
Morris Plains, NJ 07950
201-540-2000
800-492-1555
www.warner-lambert.com

S.C. Johnson & Son (Pledge, Drano, Windex, Glade)
1525 Howe St.
Racine, WI 53403
414-260-2000
800-558-5252
www.scjohnsonwax.com

SmithKline Beecham
100 Beecham Dr.
Pittsburgh, PA 15205
412-928-1000
800-456-6670
www.sb.com

SoftSoap Enterprises (Colgate-Palmolive)
300 Park Ave.
New York, NY 10022
800-221-4607
www.colgate.com

Sun Star
600 Eagle Dr.
Bensenville, IL 60106-1977
800-821-5455

3M (Scotch, Post-It)
Center Bldg., 220-2E-02
St. Paul, MN 55144-1000
612-733-1110
800-364-3577
www.3m.com

Unilever (Lever Bros., Calvin Klein, Elizabeth Arden, Helene Curtis, Diversey)
800 Sylvan Ave.
Englewood Cliffs, NJ 07632
212-888-1260
800-598-1223
www.unilever.com

Vidal Sassoon (Procter & Gamble)
P.O. Box 599
Cincinnati, OH 45202
800-543-7270
www.pg.com

Warner-Lambert (Lubriderm, Listerine, Schick)
201 Tabor Rd.
Morris Plains, NJ 07950-2693
201-540-2000
800-323-5379
www.warner-lambert.com

A Shopper's Guide to Leather Alternatives

Having trouble finding non-leather dress shoes or hiking boots for your entire family? Looking for wallets, bags, belts, briefcases, and other items made without the use of animals?

This 8-page guide offers a list of mail-order companies selling everything from non-leather baseball gloves, ice skates, rock climbing shoes, and tool belts to vegan biking gloves, Western-style boots, work boots, and much more. You'll also find suggestions about which stores tend to carry a wide selection of non-leather items.

This guide is certain to make your shopping days easier! To order, send $4 to the address below.

Other valuable guides available from VRG include:
The Vegan Diet During Pregnancy, Lactation, and Childhood $3
Guide to Food Ingredients $4
Vegetarian and Vegan Menu Items at Fast Food
and Quick Service Restaurant Chains $4

To order any of these items, please send a check or money order to The Vegetarian Resource Group, PO Box 1463, Baltimore, MD 21203 or call (410) 366-8343 weekdays between 9am and 6pm EST to charge your order with a Visa or Mastercard. You can also fax your order to (410) 366-8804 or place your order at our website: www.vrg.org

ALTERNATIVES TO LEATHER AND OTHER ANIMAL PRODUCTS

Many animals from whom skins and other body parts are obtained suffer all the horrors of factory farming, including extreme crowding and confinement, deprivation, unanesthetized castration, branding, tail-docking, and de-horning, and cruel treatment during transport and slaughter. As a result, more and more people are realizing that animal products are something we can do without.

Alternatives to leather can be found just about anywhere you might shop. But some places, such as discount shoe and variety stores, like Payless Shoe Source, Fayva, Kmart, J.C. Penney, Marshall's, and Wal-Mart, offer larger selections. Designers like Liz Claiborne, Capezio, Sam & Libby, Unlisted by Kenneth Cole, and Nike (call 1-800-344-NIKE for a current list of vegan styles) offer an array of nonleather handbags, wallets, and shoes.

For more shopping tips, send for *The Compassionate Shopper* (Beauty Without Cruelty, 175 W. 12th St., #16G, New York, NY 10011-8275) or "A Shopper's Guide to Leather Alternatives" (The Vegetarian Resource Group, P.O. Box 1463, Baltimore, MD 21203).

The following is a list of mail-order companies that specialize in nonleather clothing and accessories:

Aesop, Inc.
P.O. Box 315
N. Cambridge, MA 02140
617-628-8030

Creatureless Comforts
702 Page St.
Stoughton, MA 02072
617-344-7496

ExTredz
7015 Ordan Dr.
Unit 12-14
Mississauga, ON
L5T 1Y2 Canada
800-665-9182

Heartland Products
Box 218
Dakota City, IA 50529
800-441-4692

Ohio Hempery
7002 State Rte. 329
Guysville, OH 45735
800-BUY-HEMP

Pangea
7829 Woodmont Ave.
Bethesda, MD 20814
301-652-3181

Used Rubber USA
597 Haight St.
San Francisco, CA 94117
415-626-7855

Vegetarian Shoes
12 Gardner St.
Brighton BN1 1UP
England
011-441-273-691913

WHAT WOULD YOU DO TO SAVE AN ANIMAL?

Animals have long held a special place in my heart—their companionship has always been very important to me. That's why it distresses me to tell you that tens of thousands of animals are suffering needlessly.

They desperately need help—and organizations like PETA.

Since 1980, People for the Ethical Treatment of Animals has become this nation's most effective advocate in behalf of animal protection. The people at PETA are committed to exposing and stopping animal cruelty—especially in laboratories.

It feels great to use my voice for animals. Please join me and contact PETA today. *You* can help save animals, too.

For more information on how you can become part of this vital work, write: PETA, 501 Front St., Norfolk, VA 23510, or call 757-622-PETA.

PeTA

Rue

Health Charities: Helping or Hurting?

When you donate to a charity, do you know where the money actually goes? Could your gift be contributing to animal suffering?

Some health charities ask for donations to help people with diseases and disabilities yet spend the money to bankroll horrific experiments on dogs, rabbits, rats, mice, primates, hamsters, pigs, ferrets, frogs, fish, guinea pigs, sheep, birds, and other animals. While human health needs cry out for attention and so many people are going without medical care, animal experimentation enriches laboratories and scientists but drains money from relevant and effective projects that could really help save lives.

Healing Without Hurting

Instead of pillaging animals' bodies for cures for human diseases, compassionate charities focus their research where the best hope of treatment lies: with humans.

They realize that animal experiments are unnecessary, unreliable, and sometimes dangerously misleading. Enormous variations exist among rats, rabbits, dogs, pigs, and human beings, and meaningful scientific conclusions cannot be drawn about one species by studying another. Non-animal methods provide a more accurate method of testing and can be interpreted more objectively.

Compassionate, modern charities know that we can improve treatments through up-to-date, non-animal methods, and they fund only non-animal research, leading to real progress in the prevention and treatment of disease—without starving, crippling, burning, poisoning, or cutting open animals.

Health Charities That Don't Test on Animals

What Types of Charities Are on the "Don't Test" List?

Health charities and service organizations that do not conduct or fund experiments on animals are included on the "don't test" list. These organizations deal with human health issues ranging from birth defects to heart disease to substance abuse. Some fund non-animal research to find treatments and cures for diseases and disabilities while others provide services and direct care to people living with physical or mental ailments.

How Does a Charity Get on the List?

Charities that are listed have signed PETA's Statement of Assurance certifying that neither they nor their affiliated organizations conduct or fund any experiments on animals and will not do so in the future. Those marked with an asterisk are presently observing a moratorium on (i.e., current suspension of) animal experiments.

Please contact PETA if you know the address of a charity that is not listed, including local health service organizations. PETA will be happy to inquire about a charity's animal-testing policy, but we also encourage you to inquire, as it is important that charities hear directly from compassionate citizens who are opposed to animal testing.

* * *

The following health charities and service organizations DO NOT conduct or fund animal experiments. They may deal with several issues, including nonhealth-related issues, but they are listed according to their primary health focus. For more information on the programs and activities of an organization, please contact the organization.

AIDS/HIV

Charlotte HIV/AIDS Network, Inc. (CHAN)
P.O. Box 4229
Port Charlotte, FL 33949-4229
941-625-6650
941-625-AIDS

Chicago House
1925 N. Clayburn, Suite 401
Chicago, IL 60614
312-248-5200

Children's Immune Disorder
16888 Greenfield Rd.
Detroit, MI 48235-3707
313-837-7800

Concerned Citizens for Humanity
3580 Main St., Suite 115
Hartford, CT 06120-1121
860-560-0833

Design Industries Foundation Fighting AIDS (DIFFA)
150 W. 26th St., Suite 602
New York, NY 10001
212-645-0534

Health Cares Exchange Initiative, Inc.
P.O. Box 31
The State House
Boston, MA 02133
617-499-7780

Joshua Tree Feeding Program, Inc.
P.O. Box 7056
Phoenix, AZ 85011-7056
602-264-0223

Loving Arms
P.O. Box 3368
Memphis, TN 38173
901-725-6730

Miracle House
P.O. Box 30931
New York, NY 10011-0109
212-367-9281

Phoenix Shanti Group, Inc.
2020 W. Indian School Rd. #50
Phoenix, AZ 85015
602-279-0008

Project Open Hand
2720 17th St.
San Francisco, CA 94110
800-551-MEAL
www.openhand.org

Puerto Rico Community Network for Clinical Research on AIDS
One Stop Station, #30
P.O. Box 70292
San Juan, PR 00936-8292
809-753-9443

Santa Fe Cares
P.O. Box 1255
Santa Fe, NM 87504-1255
505-989-9255
www.santafecares.org

Texarkana AIDS Project, Inc. (TAP)
P.O. Box 3243
4425 Jefferson, Suite 107
Texarkana, AR 75504

ARTHRITIS

Arthritis Fund aka The Rheumatoid Disease Foundation
5106 Old Harding Rd.
Franklin, TN 37064
615-646-1030
taf@telalink.net

BIRTH DEFECTS

Association of Birth Defect Children, Inc.
827 Irma Ave.
Orlando, FL 32803
800-313-2232
www.birthdefects.org

Little People's Research Fund, Inc.
80 Sister Pierre Dr.
Towson, MD 21204
800-232-5773

National Craniofacial Association
P.O. Box 11082
Chattanooga, TN 37401
800-332-2373

Puerto Rico Down Syndrome Foundation
P.O. Box 195273
San Juan, PR 00919-5273
787-268-DOWN

Warner House
1023 E. Chapman Ave.
Fullerton, CA 92831
714-441-2600

BLIND, VISUALLY IMPAIRED

American Association of the Deaf-Blind
814 Thayer Ave., Suite 302
Silver Spring, MD 20910-4500

Collier County Association for the Blind
4701 Golden Gate Pkwy.
Naples, FL 34116
941-649-1122

Connecticut Institute for the Blind/Oak Hill
120 Holcomb St.
Hartford, CT 06112-1589
860-242-2274

Cumberland County Association for the Blind
837 Robeson St.
Fayetteville, NC 28305
910-483-2719

Deaf-Blind Service Center
2366 Eastlake Ave. E.
Suite 206
Seattle, WA 98102
206-323-9178

Independence for the Blind, Inc.
1278 Paul Russell Rd.
Tallahassee, FL 32301
904-942-3658

Living Skills Center for Visually Impaired
13830-B San Pablo Ave.
San Pablo, CA 94806
510-234-4984

National Federation of the Blind, Inc.
1800 Johnson St
Baltimore, MD 21230
410-659-9314

Radio Information Service
2100 Wharton St.
Suite 140
Pittsburgh, PA 15203
412-488-3944

VISIONS/Services for the Blind and Visually Impaired
120 Wall St., 16th Fl.
New York, NY 10005
212-425-2255

Washington Volunteer Readers for the Blind
901 G St. N.W.
Washington, DC 20001
202-727-2142

BLOOD

Michigan Community Blood Centers
P.O. 1704
Grand Rapids, MI 49501-1704
800-742-6317

BURNS

Children's Burn Foundation
4929 Van Nuys Blvd.
Sherman Oaks, CA 91403
818-907-2822

CANCER

Calvary Fund, Inc.
Calvary Hospital
1740 Eastchester Rd.
Bronx, NY 10461

Cancer Care Services
605 W. Magnolia
Ft. Worth, TX 76104
817-921-0653

Cancer Prevention and Survival Fund, c/o PCRM
5100 Wisconsin Ave. N.W.
Suite 404
Washington, DC 20016
202-686-2210

Danville Cancer Association, Inc.
1225 W. Main St.
P.O. Box 2148
Danville, VA 24541
804-792-3700

Miracle House
P.O. Box 30931
New York, NY 10011-0109
212-367-9281

National Children's Cancer Society
1015 Locust, Suite 1040
St. Louis, MO 63101
314-241-1600

Quest Cancer Research
Woodbury, Harlow Rd.
Roydon, Harlow, Essex
CM19 5HF
01279 792233

Skin Cancer Foundation
245 Fifth Ave., Suite 1403
New York, NY 10016
800-754-6490

Tomorrows Children's Fund
Hackensack University Medical Center
30 Prospect Ave.
Hackensack, NJ 07601
201-996-5500

CHILDREN

Association of Birth Defect Children, Inc.
827 Irma Ave.
Orlando, FL 32803
800-313-2232
www.birthdefects.org

Children's Burn Foundation
4929 Van Nuys Blvd.
Sherman Oaks, CA 91403
818-907-2822

Children's Diagnostic Center, Inc.
2100 Pleasant Ave.
Hamilton, OH 45015

Children's Immune Disorder
16888 Greenfield Rd.
Detroit, MI 48235-3707
313-837-7800

Children's Wish Foundation International
8615 Roswell Rd.
Atlanta, GA 30350-4867
800-323-WISH

Crestwood Children's Center
2075 Scottsville Rd.
Rochester, NY 14623-2098
716-436-4442

Eagle Valley Children's Home
2300 Eagle Valley Ranch Rd.
Carson City, NV 89703
702-882-1188

Five Acres/The Boys' and Girls' Aid Society of Los Angeles
760 W. Mountain View St.
Altadena, CA 91001
818-798-6793
213-681-4827
www.5acres.org

Help Hospitalized Children's Fund
10723 Preston Dr., #132
Dallas, TX 75230-3806
214-696-4743

Miracle Flights
2756 N. Green Valley Pkwy.
Suite 115
Green Valley, NV 89014-2100
800-FLY-1711

National Children's Cancer Society
1015 Locust, Suite 1040
St. Louis, MO 63101
314-241-1600

Parents and Children Coping Together
308 W. Broad St.
Richmond, VA 23220-4219
804-225-0002
800-788-0097

Pathfinder International
9 Galen St., Suite 217
Watertown, MA 02172-4501
617-924-7200

Rainbow Kids
P.O. Box 70844
Richmond, VA 23255
804-288-0479

Tomorrows Children's Fund
Hackensack University Medical Center
30 Prospect Ave.
Hackensack, NJ 07601
201-996-5500

DEAF/HEARING-IMPAIRED

American Association of the Deaf-Blind
814 Thayer Ave., Suite 302
Silver Spring, MD 20910-4500

Be an Angel Fund
T.H. Rogers School
5840 San Felipe
Houston, TX 77057
713-917-3568

Better Hearing Institute
P.O. Box 1840
Washington, DC 20013
800-EAR-WELL
www.betterhearing.org

Chicago Hearing Society
332 S. Michigan Ave.
Suite 714
Chicago, IL 60604
312-939-6888
dhhs@lancnews.infi.net

Deaf Action Center
3115 Crestview Dr.
Dallas, TX 75235
214-521-0407

Deaf-Blind Service Center
2366 Eastlake Ave. E.
Suite 206
Seattle, WA 98102
206-323-9178

Deaf Independent Living Association, Inc.
P.O. Box 4038
Salisbury, MD 21803-4038
410-742-5052

Deaf Service Center of St. Johns County
P.O. Box 1275
St. Augustine, FL 32085-1275

Institute for Rehabilitation, Research, and Recreation, Inc.
P.O. Box 1025
Pendleton, OR 97801
541-276-2752

League for the Hard of Hearing
71 W. 23rd St.
New York, NY 10010-4162
212-741-7650
www.lhh.org

Minnesota State Academy for the Deaf
P.O. Box 308
Faribault, MN 55021
800-657-3996

DISABLED, DEVELOPMENTALLY

Achievements, Inc.
101 Mineral Ave.
Libby, MT 59923
406-293-8848

Adult Training and Habilitation Center
311 Fairlawn Ave. W.
Box 600
Winsted, MN 55395
612-485-4191

Association for Community Living
One Carando Dr.
Springfield, MA 01104-3211
413-732-0531

Burnt Mountain Center
P.O. Box 337
Jasper, GA 30143
706-692-6016

Butler Valley, Inc.
380 12th St.
Arcata, CA 95521

Career Development Center
2110 W. Delaware
Fairfield, IL 62837

Carroll Haven Achieving New Growth Experiences (CHANGE)
115 Stoner Ave.
Westminster, MD 21157-5443
410-876-2179

Community Services
452 Delaware Ave.
Buffalo, NY 14202-1515
716-883-8888

Concerned Citizens for the Developmentally Disabled
P.O. Box 725
303B S. Washington St.
Chillicothe, MO 64601
816-646-0109

Creative Employment Opportunities
50711 Wing Dr.
Shelby Twp., MI 48315
810-566-4770

DeWitt County Human Resource Center
1150 Route 54 W.
Clinton, IL 61727
217-935-9496

Eagle Valley Children's Home
2300 Eagle Valley Ranch Rd.
Carson City, NV 89703
702-882-1188

EYAS Corporation
411 Scarlet Sage St.
Punta Gorda, FL 33950
813-575-2255

Hartville Meadows
P.O. Box 1055
Hartville, OH 44632
216-877-3694

Hebron Community, Inc.
P.O. Box 11
Lawrenceville, VA 23868

Hope House Foundation
100 W. Plume St., Suite 224
Norfolk, VA 23510
757-625-6161

Horizons Specialized Services, Inc.
405 Oak St.
Steamboat Springs, CO 80477-4867
303-879-4466

Kensington Community Corporation for Individual Dignity
5425 Oxford Ave.
Philadelphia, PA 19124
215-288-9797

Mountain Valley Developmental Services
P.O. Box 338
Glenwood Springs, CO 81602
970-945-2306

Mt. Angel Training Center and Residential Services
P.O. Box 78
Mt. Angel, OR 97362
503-845-9214

New Opportunities
1400 Seventh St.
Madison, IL 62060
618-876-3178

Nia Comprehensive Center for Developmental Disabilities
1808 S. State St.
Chicago, IL 60616
312-949-1808
800-NIA-1976

Opportunities for Handicapped, Inc.
3340 Marysville Blvd.
Sacramento, CA 95838
916-925-3522

Orange County Association for the Help of Retarded Citizens
249 Broadway
Newburgh, NY 12550
914-561-0670

Outlook Nashville, Inc.
3004 Tuggle Ave.
Nashville, TN 37211
615-834-7570

Phoenix Services, Inc.
1 Cumberland St.
Lebanon, PA 17042
717-270-1222

Pleasant View Homes, Inc.
P.O. Box 426
Broadway, VA 22815
540-896-8255

Primrose Center
2733 S. Fern Creek Ave.
Orlando, FL 32806-5591
407-898-7201

Project Independence of Queens
88-11 169th St., 2nd Fl.
Jamaica, NY 11432
718-657-1739

RocVale Children's Home
4450 N. Rockton Ave.
Rockford, IL 61103
815-654-3050

San Antonio State School
P.O. Box 14700
San Antonio, TX 78214-0700
210-532-0700

Society to Aid Retarded, Inc. (S.T.A.R.)
P.O. Box 1075
Torrance, CA 90505

Southwest Human Development
202 E. Earll Dr., Suite 140
Phoenix, AZ 85012
602-266-5976

St. Joseph Home, Inc.
1226 S. Sunbury Rd.
Westerville, OH 43081-9105

Swift County Developmental Achievement Center
2135 Minnesota Ave., Bldg. 1
Benson, MN 56215
320-843-4201

DISABLED, PHYSICALLY

Access to Independence, Inc.,
1310 Mendota St.
Madison, WI 53714-1039

A+ Home Care, Inc.
8932 Old Cedar Ave. S.
Bloomington, MN 55425
800-603-7760

Creative Recreation in Special Populations, Inc. (CRISP)
P.O. Box 1086
Fort Collins, CO 80522
970-493-4454

Disabled American Veterans
P.O. Box 14301
Cincinnati, OH 45250-0301
606-441-7300

Dystonia Support System
P.O. Box 21367
Cleveland, OH 44121-0367
216-321-4137

Getabout
P.O. Box 724
New Canaan, CT 06840-0224
203-966-1881

106

Greener Globe
600 Treese Way
Roseville, CA 95678
916-774-6498

Independence Crossroads
8932 Old Cedar Ave. S.
Bloomington, MN 55425
612-854-8004

Michigan Wheelchair Athletic Association
P.O. Box 1455
Troy, MI 48099
810-979-8253
michwaa@juno.com

Mower Council for the Handicapped
111 N. Main St.
Austin, MN 55912-3404
507-433-9609

San Francisco Committee for Aid of Russian Disabled Veterans
651 11th Ave.
San Francisco, CA 94118-3612

Southwestern Independent Living Center
843 N. Main St.
Jamestown, NY 14701
716-661-3010

Special People, Inc.
Human Resources
City Hall
1420 Miner St.
Des Plaines, IL 60016

United Amputee Services
P.O. Box 4277
Winter Park, FL 32793
407-678-2920
vprice@magicnet.net

DISABLED, PHYSICALLY/ DEVELOPMENTALLY

Alaska Services for Enabling Technology
P.O. Box 6485
Sitka, AK 99835
907-747-7615

Be an Angel Fund
T.H. Rogers School
5840 San Felipe
Houston, TX 77057
713-917-3568

Carroll County Health and Home Care Services
Carroll County Complex
Ossipee, NH 03864
800-499-4171

Comprehensive Advocacy, Inc.
4477 Emerald, Suite B-100
Boise, ID 83706-2044
800-632-5125

Disability Rights Education & Defense Fund (DREDF)
2212 Sixth St.
Berkeley, CA 94710
510-644-2555

Disabled Resource Services
424 Pine St., Suite 101
Fort Collins, CO 80524-2421
970-482-2700

Families Helping Families at the Crossroads of Louisiana
P.O. Box 12964
Alexandria, LA 71315-2964
318-445-7900
800-259-7200

F.A.M.I.L.Y. One-on-One Services
P.O. Box 92
W. Jordan, UT 84084
801-268-6929

Friends of the Handicapped, Inc.
P.O. Box 29
Perkasie, PA 18944
215-257-8732

Heartland Opportunity Center
Madera Center
323 N. E St.
Madera, CA 93638-3245
209-674-8828

Hodan Center, Inc.
941 W. Fountain St.
P.O. Box 212
Mineral Point, WI 53565
608-987-3336

Humboldt Community Access and Resource Center (HCAR)
P.O. Box 2010
Eureka, CA 95502

Indiana Rehabilitation Association
P.O. Box 44174
Indianapolis, IN 46244-0174
317-264-1222

Lifegains, Inc.
1601 S. Sterling St.
P.O. Drawer 1569
Morganton, NC 28680-1569
704-255-8845

Maidstone Foundation, Inc.
1225 Broadway
New York, NY 10001
212-889-5760

Maine Independent Living Services, Inc.
424 Western Ave.
Augusta, ME 04330-6014
800-499-5434

North Country Center for Independence
159 Margaret St., Suite 202
Plattsburgh, NY 12901
518-563-9058
ncci@slic.com

Open Door, Inc.
1445 S.E. Crystal Lake Dr.
Corvallis, OR 97333
503-752-9724

Options Center for Independent Living
61 Meadowview Center
Kankakee, IL 60901
815-936-0100

Ozarks Valley Community Service, Inc. (OVCS)
135 S. Main
Ironton, MO 63650-0156
573-546-2418

POWERS Coalition
P.O. Box 618
Sterling, VA 20167

Project Independence of Eastern Connecticut
401 W. Thames St.
Unit 1601
Norwich, CT 06360
203-886-0677

Rehabilitation Center
1439 Buffalo St.
Olean, NY 14760
716-372-8909

Resource Center for Accessible Living, Inc.
602 Albany Ave.
Kingston, NY 12401
914-331-0541

Riverfront Foundation
944 Green Bay St.
La Crosse, WI 54601
608-784-9450

Rockingham Opportunities
342 Cherokee Camp Rd.
Reidsville, NC 27320
336-342-4761

Sheltered Workshop
P.O. Box 2002
Clarksburg, WV 26302-2002
304-623-3757

Society Assisted Living (SAL)
4283 Paradise Rd.
Seville, OH 44273
330-725-7041
330-336-2045

Southwest Center for Independent Living
1856 E. Cinderella
Springfield, MO 65804
800-676-7245

Specialized Training for Adult Rehabilitation (START)
20 N. 13th St.
Murphysboro, IL 62966-0938
618-687-2378

Turn Community Services
P.O. Box 1287
Salt Lake City, UT 84110-1287
801-359-8876

Victor C. Neumann Association (VCN)
2354 N. Milwaukee Ave.
Chicago, IL 60647
773-278-1124

Vocational Services, Inc. (VSI)
115 Blue Jay Dr.
Liberty, MO 64068
816-781-6292

VOLAR Center for Independent Living
8929 Viscount, Suite 101
El Paso, TX 79225
915-591-0800
Volar1@whc.net

Waukesha Training Center
300 S. Prairie
Waukesha, WI 53186
414-547-6821

Western Carolina Center Foundation, Inc.
P.O. Box 646
Morganton, NC 28680-0646
704-433-2862

Windhorse Foundation
1614 Camp Springs Rd.
Reidsville, NC 27320
910-969-9590

Workshop/Northeast Career Planning
339 Broadway
Menards, NY 12204
518-463-8051

ELDERLY

Aging & Disabled Services, Inc.
811 S. Palmer Ave.
Box 142
Georgiana, AL 36033

Beth Haven
2500 Pleasant St.
Hannibal, MO 63401
573-221-6000

Carroll County Health and Home Care Services
Carroll County Complex
Ossipee, NH 03864
800-499-4171

Creative Recreation in Special Populations, Inc. (CRISP)
P.O. Box 1086
Fort Collins, CO 80522
970-493-4454

DARTS
1645 Marthaler La.
W. St. Paul, MN 55118
612-455-1560

Getabout
P.O. Box 224
New Canaan, CT 06840-0224
203-966-1881

Prairie Mission Retirement Village
242 Carroll St.
R.R. 1, Box 1Z
St. Paul, KS 66771
316-449-2400

Project Independence of Eastern Connecticut
401 W. Thames St.
Unit 1601
Norwich, CT 06360
203-886-0677

Wesley Heights
580 Long Hill Ave.
Shelton, CT 06484
203-929-5396

EMOTIONAL, BEHAVIORAL DISORDERS

AIM Center
1903 McCallie Ave.
Chattanooga, TN 37404
615-624-4800

Burke Foundation
20800 Farm Rd. 150 W.
Driftwood, TX 78619
512-858-4258

Crestwood Children's Center
2075 Scottsville Rd.
Rochester, NY 14623-2098
716-436-4442

Federation of Families for Children's Mental Health
1021 Prince St.
Alexandria, VA 22314-2971
703-864-7710
www.ffcmh.org

Lake Whatcom Center
3400 Agate Heights
Bellingham, WA 98226
360-676-6000

Parents and Children Coping Together
308 W. Broad St.
Richmond, VA 23220-4219
804-225-0002
800-788-0097

Rimrock Foundation
1231 N. 29th St.
Billings, MT 59101
800-227-3953

Staten Island Mental Health Society, Inc.
669 Castleton Ave.
Staten Island, NY 10301
718-442-2225

Timberlawn Psychiatric Research Foundation, Inc.
P.O. Box 270789
Dallas, TX 75227-0789
214-388-0451

TRANSACT Health Systems of Central Pennsylvania
90 Beaver Dr.
DuBois, PA 15801
814-371-0414

Youth Services for Oklahoma County
201 N.E. 50th St.
Oklahoma City, OK 73105-1811
405-235-7537

EPILEPSY

Epilepsy Association of the Sooner State
2405 N.W. 39th St. Expwy.
Suite 200J
Oklahoma City, OK 73112
405-521-1018

HOME CARE/MEALS

Bronx Home Care Services, Inc.
3956 Bronxwood Ave.
Bronx, NY 10466
718-231-6292

Mobile Meals, Inc.
368 S. Main St.
Akron, OH 44311-1014
330-376-7717
800-TLC-MEAL

KIDNEY

***American Kidney Fund**
6110 Executive Blvd.
Suite 1010
Rockville, MD 20852
800-638-8299
www.arbon.com/kidney/home.htm

MISCELLANEOUS

American Fund for Alternatives to Animal Research
175 W. 12th St., Suite 16G
New York, NY 10011-8220
212-989-8073

American Spinal Research Foundation
900 E. Tasman Dr.
San Jose, CA 95134
408-944-6066

Colostomy Society of New York
G.P.O. Box 517
New York, NY 10016
212-221-1246

***Endometriosis Association**
8585 N. 76th Place
Milwaukee, WI 53223
414-355-2200

Floating Hospital
Pier 11, East River at Wall St.
New York, NY 10005
212-514-7440

Greater Erie Eye and Organ Bank, Inc.
5015 Richmond St.
Erie, PA 16509-1949
814-866-3545

MCS Referral and Resources (Multiple Chemical Sensitivity)
508 Westgate Rd.
Baltimore, MD 21229-2343
410-448-3319
donnaya@rtk.net

MEA Health Care
43-576 Washington St.
Palm Desert, CA 92260
619-345-2696
http://www.psdesert.com/MEA/

National Stuttering Project
5100 E. LaPalma Ave.
Suite 208
Anaheim Hills, CA 92807
714-693-7480
800-364-1677

Southeast Vitiligo Research Foundation, Inc.
P.O. Box 7540
Clearwater, FL 34618
813-461-3899

Thyroid Society
7515 S. Main St., Suite 545
Houston, TX 77030
800-THYROID
www.the-thyroid-society.org

Transplantation Society of Michigan
2203 Platt Rd.
Ann Arbor, MI 48104
800-247-7250

Vulvar Pain Foundation
P.O. Drawer 177
Graham, NC 27253
910-226-0704

PARALYSIS

Spinal Cord Injury Network International
3911 Princeton Dr.
Santa Rosa, CA 95405
800-548-CORD
www.sonic.net/~spinal/
spinal@sonic.net

STROKE

Palm Springs Stroke Activity Center
P.O. Box 355
Palm Springs, CA 92263-0355
619-323-7676
psstrkcntr@aol.com

Stroke Survivors Support Group of Pueblo
710½ E. Mesa Ave.
Pueblo, CO 81006
719-583-8498

SUBSTANCE ABUSE

Center for Creative Alternatives
661 Hamilton, Rm. 600
Costa Mesa, CA 92627
714-437-9535

Family Service Association
31 W. Market St.
Wilkes-Barre, PA 18701-1304
717-823-5144

Friendly Hand Foundation
347 S. Normandie Ave.
Los Angeles, CA 90020
213-389-9964

Highland Waterford Center, Inc.
4501 Grange Hall Rd.
Holly, MI 48442
810-634-0140

Prevention of Alcohol Problems, Inc.
4616 Longfellow Ave. S.
Minneapolis, MN 55407
612-729-3047

Samaritan Recovery Community, Inc.
319 S. Fourth St.
Nashville, TN 37206
615-244-4802

TRAUMA/INJURY

Brain Injury Association of Florida, Inc.
201 E. Sample Rd.
Pompano Beach, FL 33064
954-786-2400

Trauma Foundation
San Francisco General Hospital
Bldg. 1, Rm. 1, 1001 Protrero
San Francisco, CA 94110
415-821-8209

VETERANS

American Veteran's Relief Fund, Inc.
5930E Royal La.
Dallas, TX 75230-3849
214-696-3784

Disabled American Veterans
P.O. Box 14301
Cincinnati, OH 45250-0301
606-441-7300

Help Hospitalized Veterans
2065 Kurtz St.
San Diego, CA 92110
619-291-5846

San Francisco Committee for Aid of Russian Disabled Veterans
651 11th Ave.
San Francisco, CA 94118-3612

GOOD **INTENTIONS** ARE **NOT** GOOD **ENOUGH**!

Be a Caring Consumer... Choose Cruelty-Free!

HEALTH CHARITIES THAT TEST ON ANIMALS

What Types of Charities Are on the "Do Test" List?

Health charities that conduct or fund experiments on animals are included on the "do test" list. These organizations deal with human health issues ranging from lung cancer to drug addiction to blindness. While some do have relevant and effective projects that help improve lives, all of them drain money away from these projects and into cruel experiments on animals. They starve, cripple, burn, poison, and slice open animals to study human diseases and disabilities. Such experiments have no practical benefit to anyone. They are unnecessary, unreliable, and sometimes dangerously misleading. "Enormous variations exist among rats, rabbits, dogs, pigs, and human beings, and meaningful scientific conclusions cannot be drawn about one species by studying another," says Neal Barnard, M.D. "Non-animal methods provide a more accurate method of testing and can be interpreted more objectively."

What Can Be Done to Stop Charities From Experimenting on Animals?

Many charities know that we can improve treatments through modern, non-animal methods, and they fund only non-animal research, leading to real progress in the prevention and treatment of disease. The next time you receive a donation request from a health charity, ask if it funds animal tests. Let charities know that you only give to organizations that alleviate suffering, not contribute to it.

* * *

Please note that most colleges and universities have laboratories that conduct animal experiments for health and other purposes. If you would like to know whether a specific school has an animal laboratory, please contact PETA. For information on the experiments being conducted and to voice your opinion, please contact the school.

* * *

The following health charities and service organizations DO conduct or fund animal experiments. They may deal with several issues, including nonhealth-related issues, but they are listed according to their primary health focus. Listed in parentheses are affiliated organizations that may or may not fund animal experiments. For more information on the programs and activities of an organization, please contact the organization or PETA.

AIDS/HIV

American Foundation for
AIDS Research (AMFAR),
733 Third Ave., 12th Fl.
New York, NY 10017
800-39-AMFAR

Pediatric AIDS Foundation
1311 Colorado Ave.
Santa Monica, CA 90404
310-395-9051

ALZHEIMER'S DISEASE

Alzheimer's Association
919 N. Michigan Ave.
Suite 1000
Chicago, IL 60611-1676
312-335-8700

Alzheimer's Disease
Research
15825 Shady Grove Rd.
Suite 140
Rockville, MD 20850
800-437-AHAF

ARTHRITIS

Arthritis Foundation
1330 W. Peachtree St.
Atlanta, GA 30309
404-872-7100

BIRTH DEFECTS

March of Dimes Birth
Defects Foundation
1275 Mamaroneck Ave.
White Plains, NY 10605
914-997-4504

Muscular Dystrophy
Association
3300 E. Sunrise Dr.
Tucson, AZ 85718-3208
800-572-1717

Shriners Hospitals for
Crippled Children
International Shrine
Headquarters
2900 Rocky Point Dr.
Tampa, FL 33607
813-281-0300

United Cerebral Palsy
1660 L St. N.W., Suite 700
Washington, DC 20036
202-776-0406

BLIND, VISUALLY IMPAIRED

Foundation Fighting
Blindness
Executive Plaza One
11350 McCormick Rd.
Suite 800
Hunt Valley, MD 21031-1014
410-785-1414

Massachusetts Lions Eye
Research Fund (Lions Club
International Foundation)
118 Allen St.
Hampden, MA 01036
413-566-3756

Research to Prevent
Blindness
645 Madison Ave., 21st Fl.
New York, NY 10022-1010
800-621-0026

BLOOD

American Red Cross
430 17th St. N.W.
Washington, DC 20006
202-737-8300

Leukemia Society of
America
600 Third Ave.
New York, NY 10016
212-573-8484

National Hemophilia
Foundation
110 Greene St.
Suite 303
New York, NY 10012
212-219-8180

BURNS

Shriners Burn Institute
International Shrine
Headquarters
2900 Rocky Point Dr.
Tampa, FL 33607
813-281-0300

CANCER

American Cancer Society
1599 Clifton Rd. N.E.
Atlanta, GA 30329
404-320-3333

American Institute for
Cancer Research
1759 R St. N.W.
Washington, DC 20009
202-328-7744

Cancer Research Foundation of America
200 Daingerfield Rd.
Suite 200
Alexandria, VA 22314
703-836-4412

City of Hope
208 W. Eighth St.
Los Angeles, CA 90014
213-626-4611

Leukemia Society of
America
600 Third Ave.
New York, NY 10016
212-573-8484

Memorial Sloan-Kettering
Cancer Center
1275 York Ave.
New York, NY 10021
212-639-2000

National Foundation for
Cancer Research
7315 Wisconsin Ave.
Suite 500W
Bethesda, MD 20814
800-321-2873

Nina Hyde Center for Breast
Cancer Research
Lombardi Cancer Research
Center
3800 Reservoir Rd. N.W.
Washington, DC 20007
202-687-4597

St. Jude Children's Research Hospital
501 St. Jude Place
Memphis, TN 38105
901-522-9733

CHILDREN

Boys Town National Research Hospital
555 N. 30th St.
Omaha, NE 68131
402-498-6511

Juvenile Diabetes Foundation International
120 Wall St.
New York, NY 10005-4001
800-JDF-CURE
www.jdfcure.com

Pediatric AIDS Foundation
1311 Colorado Ave.
Santa Monica, CA 90404
310-395-9051

Shriners Hospitals for Crippled Children
International Shrine Headquarters
2900 Rocky Point Dr.
Tampa, FL 33607
813-281-0300

Society for Pediatric Pathology
6278 Old McLean Village Dr.
McLean, VA 22101
703-556-9222

St. Jude Children's Research Hospital
501 St. Jude Place
Memphis, TN 38105
901-522-9733

Sudden Infant Death Syndrome Alliance
1314 Bedford Ave.
Suite 210
Baltimore, MD 21208
800-221-SIDS

DEAF/HEARING-IMPAIRED

Boys Town National Research Hospital
555 N. 30th St.
Omaha, NE 68131
402-498-6511

DIABETES

American Diabetes Association
1660 Duke St.
Alexandria, VA 22314
703-549-1500

Joslin Diabetes Center
One Joslin Place
Boston, MA 02215
617-732-2400

Juvenile Diabetes Foundation International
120 Wall St.
New York, NY 10005-4001
800-JDF-CURE
www.jdfcure.com

ELDERLY

American Federation for Aging Research
1414 Ave. of the Americas
18th Fl.
New York, NY 10019
212-752-2327

EMOTIONAL/BEHAVIORAL DISORDERS

National Alliance for Research of Schizophrenia and Depression
60 Cutter Mill Rd.
Suite 200
Great Neck, NY 11021
516-829-0091

National Alliance for the Mentally Ill
200 N. Glebe Rd.
Suite 1015
Arlington, VA 22203-3754
703-524-7600

EPILEPSY

Epilepsy Foundation of America
4351 Garden City Dr.
Suite 500
Landover, MD 20785
301-459-3700

HEART

American Heart Association
7272 Greenville Ave.
Dallas, TX 75231-4596
214-373-6300

Coronary Heart Disease Research
15825 Shady Grove Rd.
Suite 140
Rockville, MD 20850
800-437-AHAF

KIDNEY

National Kidney Foundation
30 E. 33rd St.
New York, NY 10016
212-889-2210

LUNG

American Lung Association
1740 Broadway
New York, NY 10019
212-315-8700

MISCELLANEOUS

American Leprosy Missions
1 ALM Way
Greenville, SC 29601
800-543-3135
www.leprosy.org

Amyotrophic Lateral Sclerosis Association
21021 Ventura Blvd.
Suite 321
Woodland Hills, CA 91364
818-340-7500

Crohn's & Colitis Foundation of America
386 Park Ave. S.
New York, NY 10016-8804
800-932-8804
www.ccfa.org

Cystic Fibrosis Foundation
6931 Arlington Rd.
Bethesda, MD 20814
800-FIGHT-CF

Families of Spinal Muscular Atrophy
P.O. Box 196
Libertyville, IL 60048-0196
800-886-1762
www.fsma.org
sma@interaccess.com

Huntington's Disease Society of America
744 Dulaney Valley Rd.
Suite 17
Towson, MD 21204
410-823-8766

International Foundation for Gastrointestinal Disorders
P.O. Box 17864
Milwaukee, WI 53217
414-964-1799

National Headache Foundation
428 W. St. James Place, 2nd Fl.
Chicago, IL 60614-2750
800-843-2256

National Multiple Sclerosis Society
733 Third Ave., 6th Fl.
New York, NY 10017-3288
212-986-3240

National Psoriasis Foundation
6600 S.W. 92nd Ave.
Suite 300
Portland, OR 97223-7195
503-244-7404

Tourette Syndrome Association
42-40 Bell Blvd.
Bayside, NY 11361-2820
800-237-0717
tourette@ix.netcom.com

PARALYSIS

American Paralysis Foundation
500 Morris Ave.
Springfield, NJ 07081
201-379-2690

Eastern Paralyzed Veterans Association
7 Mill Brook Rd.
Wilton, NH 03086
603-654-5511

Miami Project to Cure Paralysis
P.O. Box 016960, R-48
Miami, FL 33101
305-243-6001

Paralyzed Veterans of America
801 18th St. N.W.
Washington, DC 20006-3715
202-872-1300

PARKINSON'S DISEASE

American Parkinson Disease Association
1250 Hylan Blvd.
Staten Island, NY 10305
800-223-2732

National Parkinson Foundation
1501 N.W. Ninth Ave.
Miami, FL 33136
800-327-4545

Parkinson's Disease Foundation
710 W. 168th St.
New York, NY 10032-9982
212-923-4700

United Parkinson Foundation
833 W. Washington Blvd.
Chicago, IL 60607
312-733-1893

STROKE

National Stroke Association
96 Inverness Dr. E., Suite I
Englewood, CO 80112-5112
800-STROKES

VETERANS

Eastern Paralyzed Veterans Association
7 Mill Brook Rd.
Wilton, NH 03086
603-654-5511

Paralyzed Veterans of America
801 18th St. N.W.
Washington, DC 20006-3715
202-872-1300

PETA CHECKS

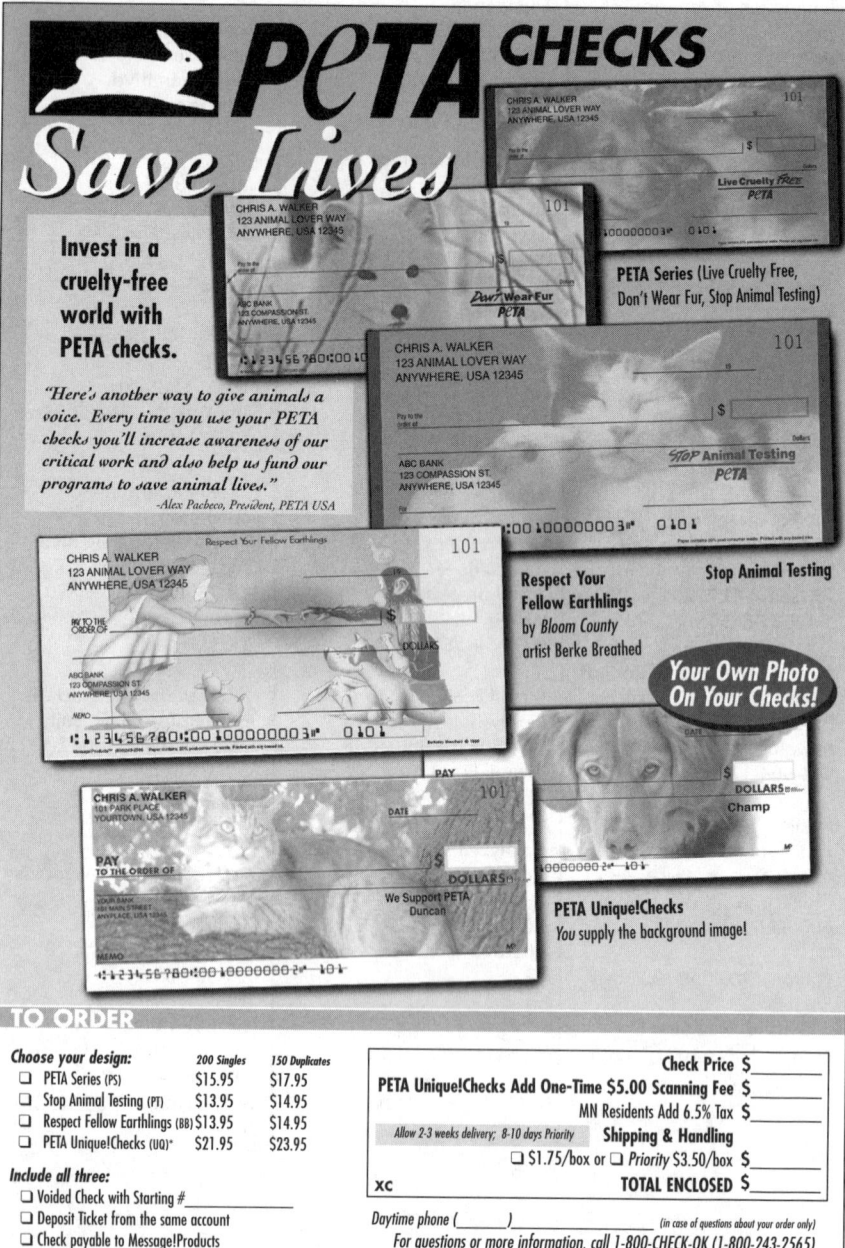

Save Lives

Invest in a cruelty-free world with PETA checks.

"Here's another way to give animals a voice. Every time you use your PETA checks you'll increase awareness of our critical work and also help us fund our programs to save animal lives."
-Alex Pacheco, President, PETA USA

PETA Series (Live Cruelty Free, Don't Wear Fur, Stop Animal Testing)

Respect Your Fellow Earthlings by *Bloom County* artist Berke Breathed

Stop Animal Testing

Your Own Photo On Your Checks!

PETA Unique!Checks
You supply the background image!

TO ORDER

Choose your design:	200 Singles	150 Duplicates
❏ PETA Series (PS)	$15.95	$17.95
❏ Stop Animal Testing (PT)	$13.95	$14.95
❏ Respect Fellow Earthlings (BB)	$13.95	$14.95
❏ PETA Unique!Checks (UQ)*	$21.95	$23.95

Include all three:
- ❏ Voided Check with Starting #_____
- ❏ Deposit Ticket from the same account
- ❏ Check payable to Message!Products

*For Unique!Checks, supply an *original* photograph. A one-time $5.00 scanning fee applies. Horizontal photos with light background colors preferred. Colors may vary. Clearly indicate a return address for the photo. Include up to 6 words as a slogan to appear above the signature line area. Add one week to delivery times listed here.

Check Price $_____
PETA Unique!Checks Add One-Time $5.00 Scanning Fee $_____
MN Residents Add 6.5% Tax $_____

Allow 2-3 weeks delivery; 8-10 days Priority **Shipping & Handling**
❏ $1.75/box or ❏ Priority $3.50/box $_____

XC **TOTAL ENCLOSED** $_____

Daytime phone (____)_____ *(in case of questions about your order only)*
For questions or more information, call **1-800-CHECK-OK (1-800-243-2565)**

Send complete order to:
Message!Products • P.O. Box 64800 • St. Paul, MN 55164-0800
or fax to: 1-800-790-6684 *(your checking account will be automatically debited)*
Order online! http://www.messagecheck.com

ABRA
THERAPEUTIC PERSONAL CARE

To receive your
ABRA Body Care Sampler
call 800-745-0761 extension 3004

APOTHECARY SHOPPE

Offering a wide selection of Aromatherapy, Herbal Medicine, and Homeobotanical Products and much more to incorporate into your everyday life!!

10% OFF YOUR FIRST ORDER

For a **FREE CATALOG** contact:
PO Box 57, Lake Oswego, OR 97034
call (800) 487-8839   fax (503) 636-0706
email achs@herbed.com   www.herbed.com

AUBREY ORGANICS
GREEN TEA

GREEN TEA...hair and skin therapy. Five new hair and skin products with Japanese powdered green tea, high in free-radical scavenging antioxidants, and certified organic aloe vera. 100% natural formulas. Sunscreen moisturizer also contains ginkgo extract–a powerful anti-wrinkle botanical.

To receive a Green Tea Sampler of trial size 1/2 oz. bottles for just $6.00, call 1-800-Aubrey H (1-800-282-7394). A $40 value regular size. Plus free Natural Ingredients Dictionary.

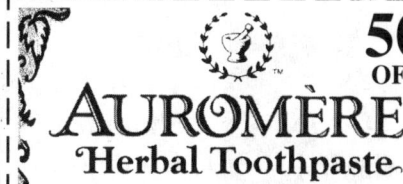

AUROMÈRE
Herbal Toothpaste

50¢ OFF

ORIGINAL * MINT-FREE * FRESHMINT
Ayurvedic Formula with Neem & Peelu

TO DEALER: Coupon will be redeemed for face value plus 8¢ handling if it has been accepted by you in accordance with the offer stated above. Invoices providing purchase of sufficient stock to cover coupon quantities must be shown upon request. Customer must pay sales tax, void if use is restricted, prohibited, or taxed. One coupon per customer. Cash value 1/100th of 1¢. To redeem, mail to: AUROMERE, 2621 W. Hwy. 12, LODI, CA 95242.

MANUFACTURER'S COUPON   Expiration Date 9/30/99

The Australasian COLLEGE of HERBAL STUDIES

Enhance your Career & Self Development
Choose from one of our 13 Natural Healing modalities.
Certificate & Diploma
Homestudy & Residential
Programs available!!

For a **FREE CATALOG** contact:
PO Box 57, Lake Oswego, OR 97034
call (800) 487-8839   fax (503) 636-0706
email achs@herbed.com   www.herbed.com

Take 15% off
your next purchase
with this coupon

BETTER BOTANICALS®
HERBAL ■ BALANCING ■ PURE
Toll-free: (888) bbherbs; www.betterbotanicals.com

BIOGIME®
Simply Beautiful Skin

1-800-338-8784
FREE SAMPLE & BROCHURE

ANY PURCHASE
DIRECT FROM
BRONZO SENSUALÉ

$5.00 OFF

www.bronzosensuale.com
(800) 991-2226 • (305) 531-2992

OFFER GOOD FOR ONE PURCHASE ONLY.
NON-APPLICABLE WITH OTHER OFFERS.

CARING CONSUMER PROJECT	**PETA'S 1999 Shopping Guide for Caring Consumers** Redeemable through company only.
CARING CONSUMER PROJECT	**PETA'S 1999 Shopping Guide for Caring Consumers** Redeemable through company only.
CARING CONSUMER PROJECT	**PETA'S 1999 Shopping Guide for Caring Consumers** Redeemable through company only.
CARING CONSUMER PROJECT	**PETA'S 1999 Shopping Guide for Caring Consumers** Redeemable through company only.
CARING CONSUMER PROJECT	**PETA'S 1999 Shopping Guide for Caring Consumers** Redeemable through company only.
CARING CONSUMER PROJECT	**PETA'S 1999 Shopping Guide for Caring Consumers** Redeemable through company only.
CARING CONSUMER PROJECT	**PETA'S 1999 Shopping Guide for Caring Consumers** Redeemable through company only.
CARING CONSUMER PROJECT	**PETA'S 1999 Shopping Guide for Caring Consumers** Redeemable through company only.

CAERAN® Gift Certificate

5 Five Dollars — 5 Five Dollars

Caring And Environmentally Responsible And Nurturing

Please redeem this coupon through: 1-800-563-2974

How did you receive this Gift Certificate? (Check appropriate box)
☐ Fundraiser ☐ School ☒ Gift
Date PeTA Expiry Date N/A

Minimum purchase $70.00. Not valid during fundraising events or in conjunction with any other coupons or offers.
25 Penny Lane, Brantford, Ontario • (519) 751-0513 • 1-800-563-2974

Retailer of quality Household Products, Beauty & Skin Care

$3.00 OFF COUPON

The Caring Catalog

7678 Sagewood Drive
Huntington Beach, CA 92648
(714) 842-0454

COSMETICS & CLEANERS • BATH & BEAUTY • TOILETRIES & MORE

Compassion Matters
2 East Fourth Street
Jamestown, NY 14701
1-800-422-6330
Cruelty-free products for men & women.
Receive 10% off your first order

Derma E®

Healthy, Younger Looking Skin...Naturally!

TO RECEIVE YOUR FREE BROCHURE & SAMPLE

MAIL THIS COUPON TO:

Derma E®
9400 Lurline Ave., #C-1
Chatsworth, CA 91311

For Questions or Comments Call: 1 (800) 521-3342
http://www.derma-e.com

Save 50¢

EARTH FRIENDLY PRODUCTS®

On any one of the following Earth Friendly Products, through the PETA Catalog;

Dishmate™, Orange Plus®, Cream Cleanser, Toilet Bowl Cleaner, Ecos®, Uni•Fresh™ and Window Kleener.

Eco-DenT® Premium Natural Oral Care

DAILYRINSE™
Ultimate Essential MouthCare™

FREE TRIAL SAMPLE
DOUBLE-YOUR-MONEY BACK DENTAL CARE COUPON

Mail Coupon to: Eco-DenT International
P.O. Box 5285 • Redwood City, CA 94063

FLEABUSTERS

"A Natural Alternative Flea Control"
Kills Fleas For One Year

10% Discount on all orders with this coupon

To order or for more information:
1-800-666-3532

The Heritage Store
YOUR GATEWAY TO HEALTH

massage lotions, herbal remedies, supplements, natural bath, dental, complexion and upper respiratory care - all recommended by Edgar Cayce.

FREE Catalog
(757) 428-0100

The Heritage Store
P.O. Box 444 • Virginia Beach, VA 23458

CARING CONSUMER PROJECT

PETA'S 1999 Shopping Guide for Caring Consumers
Redeemable through company only.

INSTANT STORE COUPON

$3.00 off on your next purchase of **Any 3 Products** from Jason Natural Cosmetics **$3.00 off**

/JĀSÖN/®
NATURAL COSMETICS
Available at Health/Natural Food stores.

Dear Retailer: We will reimburse the face value of the coupon plus 8 cents for handling to the Health Food retailers provided you accept it from your customer on the purchase of any three (3) JASON PRODUCTS. Any other application constitutes fraud. Mail the coupon to: JASON NATURAL COSMETICS, 8468 Warner Dr., Culver City, CA 90232-2484. Expires: 06/30/99 1-800-JASON-05

JA
JOHN AMICO

Hair Care Products
- Botanical Extracts
- Topical Vitamins & Minerals for the Hair

Contact Our Web Site for a
Complimentary Customized Product
Available only in Professional Salons
www.johnamico.com

La Crista

The Skin Care Specialist ... Naturally

FREE!!!

Trial Size Dewberry Lotion
Send name, address, and request to:
LaCrista, Inc.
P.O. Box 240 • Davidsonville, MD 21035

Natural • No Mineral Oil or Harsh Chemicals

CONTACT LENS SOLUTIONS

Your **PETA** coupon pays the postage
On the purchase of any two solutions
Lobob SOF/PRO CLEAN 1.3 oz. $6.60
Optimum by Lobob RGP Cleaner $9.00
Optimum by Lobob RGP C/D/S $9.00
Optimum by Lobob RGP W/RW $9.00
Send check, M.O. or call w/ VISA or M/C
California orders must include 8.25% ST
Lobob Laboratories 1440 Atteberry Lane
San Jose, CA 95131   1-800-83LOBOB

A clean lens is a comfortable lens

The Mother's Fragrances Incense & Oils

Send in this coupon for free incense sample!

Mere Cie, Inc.
1100 Soscol Ferry Rd. #3
Napa, CA 94558
Phone: (800)832-4544
web site: www.merecie.com

Natracare™
NATURAL BODYCARE FROM ENGLAND

NON-CHLORINE TAMPONS (100% COTTON) AND PADS.

Sample
191 University Blvd., Suite 294
Denver, Colorado 80206

CRUELTY-FREE SUPPLEMENTS!

- Vitamin capsules
- Mineral capsules
- Herbs in vegan capsules
- Diet supplements
- Sports supplements
- Powdered supplements

To recieve a FREE catalog & sample call: (800) 523-8899, or send coupon to:
Health USA
Attn: Catalog/Sample Request
1727 Cosmic Way, Glendale, CA 91201

Call for FREE Sample!

---

body care
shoes
ties
belts
t-shirts

pangea

chocolate
books
bags
jackets
cosmetics

7829 WOODMONT AVE., BETHESDA MD 20814
**PANGEA Vegan Products:
The Vegan Everything Store!**
Call (301) 652-3181 for catalog or visit our
website (http://www.pangeaveg.com)
$5 off your 1st order of $25 or more w/ this ad!

CARING CONSUMER PROJECT

PETA'S 1999 Shopping Guide for Caring Consumers
Redeemable through company only.

CARING CONSUMER PROJECT

PETA'S 1999 Shopping Guide for Caring Consumers
Redeemable through company only.

CARING CONSUMER PROJECT

PETA'S 1999 Shopping Guide for Caring Consumers
Redeemable through company only.

CARING CONSUMER PROJECT

PETA'S 1999 Shopping Guide for Caring Consumers
Redeemable through company only.

CARING CONSUMER PROJECT

PETA'S 1999 Shopping Guide for Caring Consumers
Redeemable through company only.

CARING CONSUMER PROJECT

PETA'S 1999 Shopping Guide for Caring Consumers
Redeemable through company only.

CARING CONSUMER PROJECT

PETA'S 1999 Shopping Guide for Caring Consumers
Redeemable through company only.

CARING CONSUMER PROJECT

PETA'S 1999 Shopping Guide for Caring Consumers
Redeemable through company only.

TRIAL OFFER

Patricia Allison

Specify Skin Type

SKIN CARE SET
(CLEANSER, TONER, MOISTURIZER)
AND
15% DISCOUNT COUPON

SEND $2.00 TO: PATRICIA ALLISON 4470 MONAHAN ROAD LA MESA, CA 91941

rainbow
Natural Body Care

NOT Tested on Animals • NO Animal Ingredients

Henna (Hair Color) • Shampoo • Conditioner • Body Oil
Body Lotion (Unscented & Oil Free) • Green Clay
Bubble Bath • Soap • Hair Spray & Gel
Featuring: Rainbow Salon Botanicals

FREE CATALOG
With $5.00 Gift Certificate

Call: 1-800-722-9595
Rainbow Research • PO Box 153
Dept P • Bohemia, NY 11716

Save $1.00 SHADOW LAKE™

On any one of the following Shadow Lake Products:

*Citra-Solv® Concentrate, Citra-Solv® RTU Spray
Air Scense™ air freshener, Orange, Lime, Vanilla
Shadow Lake™ Pure Castile Soap
Peppermint, Eucalyptus/Spearmint, Vanilla/Almond*

Limit one coupon per items specified. Void if reproduced. Retailer: Shadow Lake, Inc., P.O. Box 2597 Danbury, CT. 06713-2597, will redeem this coupon according to our redemption policy plus $0.08 handling. One coupon per purchase. Cash value 1/100¢.

$1.00 Off

any

ShiKai
DERMACEUTICAL FORMULATION

redeem at a participating retailer
limit 1 coupon per purchase

MANUFACTURER'S COUPON   EXPIRES 12/31/99

THE SOAP OPERA

We offer only 100% biodegradable, cruelty free (no animal testing) products based on earth-friendly, safe, effective ingredients, continuing our business philosophy unchanged since 1972!

**FREE CATALOG
800-251-7627**

319 STATE ST • MADISON WI 53703
(608) 251-4051 • fax (608) 251-1703
www.thesoapopera.com

TERRESSENTIALS®
"The purest of the pure."
-E magazine

ABSOLUTELY NO PETROCHEMICALS

Free catalog of the finest chemical-free natural body care on earth! Cosmetics, pet care, feminine necessities, home & garden items, books too! No artificial colors, synthetic fragrances or chemical preservatives.

2650 Old National Pike, Middletown MD 21769-8817
Phone 301 371-7333 E-mail 72760.2745@compuserve.com

10% OFF COUPON

"DAISY" Says:
The only thing that should dye for glamour is your hair!
Tish & Snooky's

MANIC PANIC®
Hair Color & Cosmetics for the *Wild at Heart*

Hair Color in more colors than the Rainbow ★ Wild Wig Stock
★ Glitters and Gems for Body, Face, Hair ★
★ Amazing Make Up ★ Claw Colors Nail Polish ★

64-66 White St. New York NY 10013 Phone(212)941-0656
Fax(212)941-0634 Email:manicnyc@aol.com Call 1(800)95MANIC

10% OFF

Crystal Orchid®

5.0 oz	*Deodorant Stone*	$9.95
3.5 oz	*Loofa Seaweed Soap*	$6.95

plus $3.50 shipping and handling

LONG LASTING

1-800-487-2633
1414 E. Libra Dr. Tempe, AZ 85283

CARING CONSUMER PROJECT

PETA'S 1999 Shopping Guide for Caring Consumers
Redeemable through company only.

For a *FREE catalog & discount coupon*, return this ad along with your name and address to:

Vermont Soapworks
76 Exchange Street
Middlebury, VT 05753
Phone: (802) 388-4302
Fax: (802) 388-7471
Web Site: www.vtsoap.com

(zia) **save $3.00**

Indulge on us!

Apply toward your first purchase of any Zia Cosmetics product. (*full size only*)

**ULTIMATES-SKIN BASICS-TREATMENTS
COLOR BASICS-SUN BASICS**

Limit one item per coupon specified. Void if reproduced, exchanged or transferred. Retailer: Zia Cosmetics 1337 Evans Avenue, San Francisco, CA 94124, 800-334-7546 will redeem this coupon according to our redemption policy plus $.08. One coupon per purchase. Cash value 1/100¢.

CARING CONSUMER PROJECT	**PETA'S 1999 Shopping Guide for Caring Consumers** Redeemable through company only.	CARING CONSUMER PROJECT	**PETA'S 1999 Shopping Guide for Caring Consumers** Redeemable through company only.

What Is PETA?

People for the Ethical Treatment of Animals (PETA) is an international nonprofit organization dedicated to exposing and eliminating all animal abuse. PETA uses public education, litigation, research and investigations, media campaigns, and involvement at the grassroots level to accomplish this goal.

With the help of our dedicated members, PETA persuades major corporations to stop testing products on animals; advocates alternatives to eating animals by promoting a vegetarian diet; and has forced the closure of federally funded animal research facilities because of animal abuses.

To help stop the exploitation and abuse of animals, become a PETA member today.

MEMBERSHIP & DONATION FORM

Enclosed is my contribution to go toward your vital work in behalf of all animals.

❑ $15   ❑ $25   ❑ $50   ❑ $100   ❑ Other $_____

(Annual membership is $15.00. Members receive PETA's *Guide to Compassionate Living* and a subscription to PETA's quarterly newsletter.)

❑ I'm already a PETA member. This is an extra donation.

Name _____

Address _____

City _____ State _____ Zip _____

Complete this form and send with your check to:

PeTA 501 Front St., Norfolk, VA 23510

Thank you from all of us at PETA.

Ask your store to carry these books:

Vegan Vittles
A collection of recipies inspired by the critters of Farm Sanctuary. Includes photos and biographies of resident animals.

$11.95

Cooking With PETA
Over 200 recipes, plus tips on replacing eggs and dairy products in cooking, using "mock meats," and cooking healthful vegan foods that kids will eat.

$14.95

Nonna's Italian Kitchen
Regional Italian culinary magic. All vegan & delicious.

$14.95

Becoming Vegetarian
Three vegetarian dieticians present the latest nutritional information for optimal health and kindness.

$15.95

Warming Up to Living Foods
Zesty, creative, nutritious dishes made from raw and living foods.

$15.95

Peaceful Palate
Quality vegan fare for the novice or veteran cook.

$15.00

or you may order directly from:
The Book Publishing Company
P.O. Box 99
Summertown, TN 38483

Or call: 1-800-695-2241
Please add $2.50 per book for shipping.